Guide
to the Museum
of the Château
de Fontainebleau

W9-COL-195

Guide to the Museum of the Château de Fontainebleau

by Jean-Pierre Samoyault
Conservateur général

Réunion
des Musées
Nationaux

Front cover:
The Horseshoe Staircase Wing

ISBN:2 - 7118 - 2454 - 3

© Editions
de la Réunion
des musées nationaux
Paris 1994
49, rue Etienne Marcel
75001 Paris

History of the buildings, gardens and interior decoration

1.
Louis VII's seal
(Paris, Archives nationales).

The Château de Fontainebleau was mentioned for the first time in 1137, in a royal charter of King Louis VII the Younger (fig. 1). Its appearance at that time can only be surmised, for all that remains today is the keep, a large square tower considerably altered. In 1259, King Louis IX (Saint Louis) founded nearby, close to the future White Horse Courtyard, a monastery-hospital which he entrusted to the Trinitarian monks, in charge of the redemption of captives. However, as the monastery buildings disappeared in the course of the 16th century, little is known of their site and layout (despite attempts made by A. Bray to imagine how they were planned (fig. 2). At the beginning of the 15th century important work was done on the château itself, if we are to give credence to a letter from Charles VII, dated 1431. The king's mother, Isabella of Bavaria, whose dower included Fontainebleau, may have had it rebuilt. Indeed, certain portions of the walls and several bays along the façades of the Oval Courtyard seem to bear traces of this construction.

2.
Conjectural plan of the Château as it was at the end of the 15th century, drawn by the architect A. Bray and published in 1935.

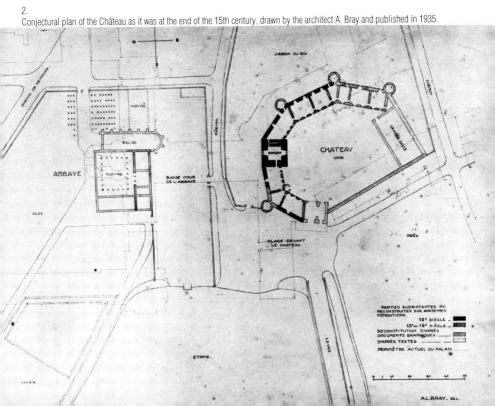

3.
Titian,
François I
(Paris, Musée
du Louvre).

The major date of modern times in the history of Fontainebleau is that of 1528, shortly after the return of François I (fig. 3) from his captivity in Madrid. It was the starting point of a virtually uninterrupted series of royal sojourns and artistic embellishments, lasting until 1870, which forged the image, both real and legendary, of Fontainebleau today. In less than twenty years, François I had the castle rebuilt and enlarged, the interiors decorated and the gardens laid out. Here he brought together prestigious paintings, sculpture, objets d'art and books, which form the nucleus of the French national collections.

In 1528, after continuing some work commissioned the previous year, the king decided to knock down the greater part of the old château and erect a new one on the former foundations (Oval Courtyard). He then resolved to retrieve some land from the Trinitarian monks, needed to enlarge the estate, and to integrate the abbey into the royal château by linking them with a gallery (the François I Gallery wing). Thus the general plan of Fontainebleau today was due to the determination of a single man and though at first it may appear to lack coherence, it becomes much more intelligible once we realise the role played by the François I Gallery wing (fig. 4) as the main articulation connecting all the other buildings.

These new constructions, executed rapidly between 1528 and 1531, using simple materials, sandstone and mortar rubble, were accompanied on the abbey side by annexes for the administrative and domestic staff around a base-court. Various outbuildings went up between 1530 and 1535: the small and large jeu de paume

courts, kennels, the keeper's lodge and pavilions in the large garden (one of which, wrongly named the Pavillon de Sully, still exists). Here brick replaced sandstone.

Throughout his reign, the king constantly made alterations to the architecture of his château. The grand staircase in the Oval or Keep Courtyard was planned in 1531 but "modified" in 1541 (today's so-called Serlio Portico) and a colonnade was placed around the courtyard. The decision to build its own chapel for the château – two superimposed chapels, according to an ancient tradition (cf. the Sainte Chapelle in Paris) – was also made in 1531, though it was not finished until 1546. In April 1534 the king ordered the erection of a terraced building alongside the François I Gallery to house the kitchens and pantries on the ground floor. During the following years the Fountain Courtyard was formed with, on one hand, the Stove Pavilion beside the pond (around 1538), linked by a lower wing to the François I Gallery and, on the other, a matching edifice, later encapsulated in the wing called the Fine Chimney Wing. About this time the lower building on the south side of the base-court of the abbey was heightened and extended to create a long gallery on the upper storey (later called the Ulysses Gallery owing to its decoration). Construction began in the last years of the reign on the loggia wing (fig. 5), between the Golden Gate and the royal chapel, but it was still uncompleted at the King's death. At the same time the abbey buildings were gradually replaced by a new wing, known today as the Horseshoe Staircase Wing.

The king also took an interest in the gardens (the pond enclosure garden planted with pinetrees, a grotto adorned with rustic figures, the Pomona Pavilion), but it was above all the interior decoration commissioned for the apartments that gave Fontainebleau its great reputation at the time. François I called on two great Italian artists: the magnificent creator of masterpieces of religious painting, the Florentine Giovanni-Battista di Jacopo, called Il Rosso (1494-1540), and Francesco Primaticcio (1504-1570), of Bolognese origin, who had been trained as a stucco decorator by

4. The Château *circa* 1540 (fresco in the François I Gallery): left, the François I Gallery Wing; right, the Golden Gate and the south wing of the Keep Courtyard.

5. Design proposed by the architect Sebastiano Serlio for the Loggia Wing to replace the south façade, *c.* 1545 (*Seventh Book of Architecture*, published in Venice, 1584, p. 97).

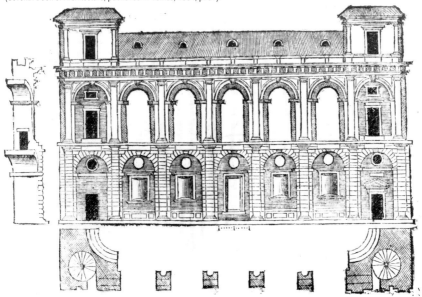

Giulio Romano in Mantua. These two artists, each surrounded by numerous assistants, were to rival in producing works of great originality, associating fresco painting with stucco sculpture and carved wood panelling. This was the First School of Fontainebleau, which was to have such a momentous influence on 16th-century French art and, thanks to engravings, on the whole of Europe. The first important undertakings concerned the King's Bedchamber (1533-1535) (fig. 6) and the Queen's Bedchamber (1534-1537), entrusted to Primaticcio, as well as the King's Gallery (1533?-c. 1539) for which Rosso was made responsible. Next came the creation of decorations for the main entrance to the château,

with the bedroom on the first floor (Primaticcio), together with those for the apartments of the Stove Pavilion (Rosso). At the death of Rosso, Primaticcio became the uncontested master of decoration at Fontainebleau and was in charge of those in the lower gallery (c. 1542), the bedroom of Madame d'Etampes, the vestibule of the Golden Gate (c. 1541-1544), the king's closet, and the baths apartment below King's Gallery, and finally the Ulysses Gallery. All these enterprises give some idea of the scope of the king's patronage of the arts and the role played by Fontainebleau in making known in France the most recent accomplishments of Italian art.

6.
Primaticcio, *Design for the Decoration of the King's Bedchamber,* c. 1533 (carried out), drawing (Paris, Musée du Louvre).

7.
François Clouet
(studio of),
Henri II
(Paris, Musée
du Louvre).

This artistic policy did not come to an end with the death of the king; it was pursued by Henri II (fig. 7) who in no way neglected Fontainebleau. The great architect Philibert Delorme became the principal superintendent of works and under his direction construction and decoration already begun were faithfully completed according to plan (monks chapel, Ulysses Gallery). Simultaneously, innovations were made: a cabinet was built for the queen, jutting out into the garden of the keeper's lodge (1548-1550); the loggia planned between the Oval Court-

yard and the King's Garden was transformed into a ballroom (around 1548-1558) and adorned with paintings executed under the direction of Primaticcio by a team of artists headed by Nicolo dell'Abbate from Modena; a great flight of steps (fig. 8), the pride of Philibert Delorme, was created near the new monks' chapel. The king himself decided to move his apartment and from 1555 had several rooms arranged in the Stove Pavilion. Carved woodwork was commissioned for the chapels (the tribune and organ case in the king's upper chapel, a rood-screen and an oratory for the king in the new great chapel), as well as for the sovereign's armoury in the Arms Pavilion. In 1558 Philibert Delorme negociated the reconstruction in ashlar of the wing situated in the Fountain Courtyard between the Stove Pavilion and the François I Gallery, but he fell out of favour at the death of King Henri II in 1559 and had to relinquish his post to Primaticcio. Thanks to the confidence accorded to Primaticcio by the queen mother, Catherine de Médicis, the pain-

8.
The first Horseshoe Staircase by the architect Philibert Delorme
(detail from an engraving in the *Deuxième volume des plus excellents bastiments de France* by J. Androuet du Cerceau, 1579).

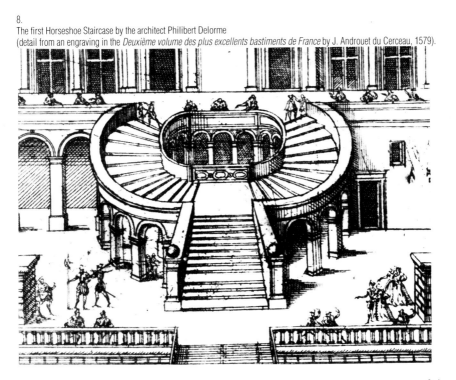

9.
François Clouet
(studio of),
Charles IX
(Paris, Musée
du Louvre).

ter-decorator became superintendent of royal buildings. For ten years, until his death in 1570, he presided over the destiny of Fontainebleau, during the reigns of François II and Charles IX (fig. 9). Whereas Delorme did not have time to give full measure of his talent, Primaticcio was able to do so by taking over, with some modifications, his predecessor's plan for the Stove Pavilion Wing

(completed in 1565 by the Base-court Staircase Pavilion) and by erecting in the Fountain Courtyard, between 1565 and 1570, the building with the great double flight of steps. The use of ashlar and the choice of a strict order for the buildings finally revolutionised the architecture of the château. The new wing begun by Primaticcio in 1565 on the Diana Garden side, in order to double the area of the royal apartments, was less original. The Bolognese artist also installed a plaster-cast horse in the base-court (hence the name of White Horse Courtyard), and built a pergola adorned with sculptures in the Queen's private garden (1561-1562), as well as a dairy in the park. He surrounded the château with a moat (1565) for defence purposes, and continued to supervise the decoration, providing the painter Nicolo dell'Abbate with cartoons for the King's

10.
General view of the Château (engraving in the *Deuxième volume des plus excellents bastiments de France* by J. Androuet du Cerceau, 1579).

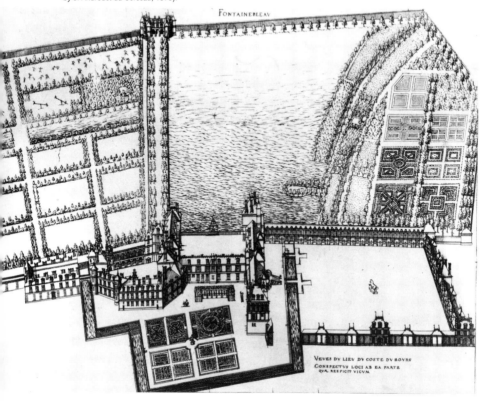

Apartment, the Queen's Dairy and the continuation of the Ulysses Gallery.

Work was not interrupted by the death of Primaticcio, though in the following years, operations no doubt slowed down owing to general circumstances and to financial problems. The absence of accounts for the whole of the end of the 16th century contributes to the obscurity concerning work undertaken at Fontainebleau at the time. Thus we can only cite with certainty the decoration of the ceiling in the King's Chamber (the first of the present-day Saint Louis Chambers) in 1572 and the placing of the ceiling in the great new hall in 1578. The 1570 plan to harmonise all the façades of the Fountain Courtyard by constructing a new terrace along the François I Gallery and facing the building in ashlar, had apparently still not materialised in 1579 (engravings by Du Cerceau) (fig. 10).

11.
François II
Pourbus,
Henri IV
(Paris, Musée
du Louvre).

It was not until the end of the Wars of Religion that Fontainebleau came to life again, under the patronage of Henri IV (fig. 11). Within a few years, the king's achievements were considerable in every field (fig. 12): architecture, landscaping and interior decoration. Although he made few changes to the buildings of the White Horse Courtyard and of the Fountain Courtyard, he improved the

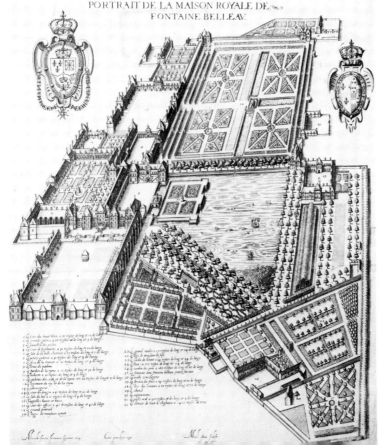

PORTRAIT DE LA MAISON ROYALE DE
FONTAINE BELLEAV.

12.
The Château
of Fontainebleau
and gardens in 1614,
engraving by
Michel Lasne from a
drawing by
Alexandre Francini.

Keep Courtyard by enlarging it and opening up a monumental domed gateway (between 1601 and 1606). Near the Queen's Garden, he created, without any preconceived plan, three brick and stone wings, advancing at right angles from the main building in a rather ornate Mannerist style – the first serving as an aviary (*c.* 1599), the second linking this aviary by way of galleries to the royal apartments (this is the wing of the Queen's Gallery and the Stags Gallery, *c.* 1600), and the third one enclosing the space (wing of the Roe Gallery, about 1601). He erected two jeu de paume courts, the new keeper's lodge (starting in 1601) and a new base-court (1606-1609). At the same time, the gardens received his careful attention. The king entrusted the landscape design to the Mollet brothers and two Florentine hydraulic engineers, the Francini brothers. Several sculptors collaborated with them. Most of the existing gardens were altered: the Pinetree Garden was adorned with clipped hedges; in the King's Main Garden, the small canals were filled in to make way for a new symmetrical layout of box-tree parterres surrounding fountains, executed in two stages about 1603 (fig. 13) and around 1608; the Queen's Garden received a fountain in honour of Diana (1603). Other gardens were created: the Pond Garden on a stone bastion surrounded by water (1594-1595), the Canal Wood, the Fruit Garden, the Mall and the Mulberry Walk beyond the Pinetree Garden. A large park was laid out around a vast canal, nearly one thousand two hundred metres long (1608-1609). Fountains were set up in all the courtyards.

13.
The Tiber Fountain created in 1603
by Thomas Francini,
engraving by Michel Lasne
in the book by Père P. Dan,
*Le Trésor des merveilles
de la maison royale de
Fontainebleau*, 1642.

14.
Ambroise Dubois,
*Fight between Tancred
and Clorinda* (Fontainebleau,
Musée national du château).

The transformations inside the castle were no less extensive. On the whole the king treated the accomplishments of his predecessors with respect, completing certain enterprises (Ulysses Gallery), restoring apartments in poor condition (Baths Apartment) and adding here and there a portrait or his monogram. In his own and the queen's apartments, two rooms were entirely redecorated: the queen's cabinet (which, apparently around 1603, was adorned with scenes from the story of Clorinda – (fig. 14) – after Tasso), and the Oval Bedroom (with illustrations of the Loves of Theagenes and Chariclea, added around 1609-1610). The king commissioned the decoration of other buildings that had gone up before his reign, but which lacked ornamentation: the great new hall was embellished with the famous Fine Chimney (fig. 15), sculpted by Mathieu Jacquet (1597-1601); in the upper keep chapel, the walls and vaulted ceiling were painted in 1608; in the monks' chapel, work on the vaulted ceiling also began in 1608. The newly erected buildings were decorated with the same profusion: the Stags Gallery and the Roe Gallery (fig. 16) dedicated to the royal forests and to hunting, the Queen's Gallery where the mythological themes of Apollo and Diana were associated with the glorification of the sovereign and the representation of his military victories. The king also had a small apartment arranged on the ground floor of the keeper's lodge, adorned with landscapes. These decorations were carried out by teams of artists under the direction of several well-known figures: Toussaint Dubreuil, who died prematurely

15.
The Fine Chimney,
detail of an elevation
of the Château de Fontainebleau
drawn by the architect
François Dorbay, 1676
(Paris, Archives nationales).

16.
Stags Gallery,
decor restituted by
Antoine-Laurent Castellan,
print published in 1840.

in 1602, the Dutchman Jean d'Hoey, Ambroise Dubois from Antwerp, Martin Fréminet, a Parisian, and Louis Poisson from Normandy. Among the sculptors, we should mention Barthélemy Tremblay, Thomas Thourin, François de La Vacquerie. The work executed over a period of about fifteen years was considerable and, according to Father Dan, the 17th-century historian of the château, the king spent the sum of two million four hundred and forty thousand eight hundred and fifty *livres*. Fontainebleau was now truly at its zenith; it had become a highly prestigious monument that would never cease to be admired.

17.
Philippe de Champaigne,
Louis XIII
(Paris, Musée
du Louvre).

The reign of Louis XIII (fig. 17) represented a period of stability for the royal residence. Apart from the reconstruction in the shape of a horseshoe of the flight of steps in the base-court by the architect Jean Androuet du Cerceau (1632-1634), little architectural work of importance was undertaken: the *Surintendance des Finances* (1632), an oratory for the king jutting on to the Queen's Garden (1642-1643). Inside, the only major operation was the completion of the decoration in the chapels. For the upper chapel, six large pictures were commissioned from Ambroise Dubois in 1612 and finished after 1631 (fig. 18). Work on the Trinity Chapel, interrupted at an unknown date, was resumed only in 1628, and completed in 1642. The Horseshoe Vestibule on the first floor,

18.
Upper Saint Saturnin Chapel
at the beginning of the 19th century,
watercolour drawing by the architect J.-F.-A. Robit
(Fontainebleau, Bibliothèque municipale).

20.
The great parterre and the Cascades Fountain
at the time of Louis XIV,
engraving by Israël Silvestre, 1678.

18

leading to the chapel tribune, was decorated in 1639, just when the walls of the lower keep chapel were painted (by Claude d'Hoey) and garnished with wood panelling (by Gobert).

After the death of Louis XIII, the Queen Regent Anne d'Autriche, urged by the Superintendent of buildings, Sublet des Noyers, was determined to bring to an end the parcimonious policy which had characterised the reign of her husband, and launched forth on a programme of embellishments. She decided to refurbish her apartment which she found old-fashioned, without touching the Clorinda Room. In 1644, her large cabinet, her bedchamber and the Emperors Chamber were given new wood panelling and ceilings. Simon Vouet decorated the vestibule of the Diana Gallery. Soon after, the king's bedchamber and the Saint Louis Chamber were transformed. The queen also asked Le Nôtre to start work on her garden, while she brought from Paris sculptures and paintings from the Cardinal de Richelieu's collection, bequeathed to the king. In 1654, whilst she was planning the future marriage of Louis XIV (fig. 19), the queen began work on the Stove Pavilion Wing. She commissioned Le Vau to erect a

19.
René-Antoine Houasse,
Louis XIV
(Versailles, Musée
national du château).

domed pavilion, on the terrace overlooking the pond, giving her direct access to the Ulysses Gallery. Most of the arrangements in this wing actually date from the years 1659-1664. Anne d'Autriche then changed the disposition of the rooms and had almost all the decorations renovated. Of Henri II's former apartment, she kept only the cabinet on the terrace and the ceiling of the king's bedchamber which was moved to her antechamber. The painters, Cotelle, Erard and Mauperché, took part in these important decorations. The fact that, during the same years, King Louis XIV had a pool with cascades installed by Le Nôtre (1661-1662) (fig. 20) and asked the famous landscape designer to remodel the Tiber Parterre (1661-1665), seemed to presage his desire

20

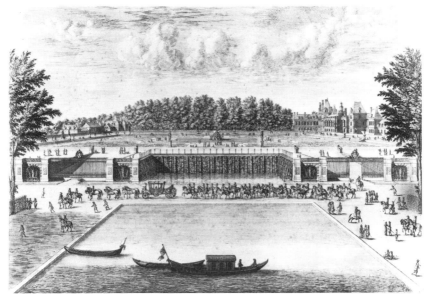

to leave his personal mark on the dwelling of his ancestors. Yet, out of respect for the past, and also because of the great projects for Versailles that absorbed his attention, Louis XIV left Fontainebleau almost intact. Between 1678 and 1685 a few new constructions were added to the outbuildings and the staff lodgings (great stables, the house for the superintendent of buildings, mansions for the secretaries of state), while improvements were made on the great park (new basins in the meadow). In 1686, an apartment was installed for Madame de Mainte-

non. In 1697 the Baths Apartment of François I was definitively condemned. Thereafter, to accommodate new lodgings, Mansart created a new wing in the keeper's lodge courtyard, obscuring the Queen's Gallery on the east side (1701). It was not until the end of the reign though, that the next important changes took place (fig. 21): in the years 1713-1714, the Pond Garden was dug up, the Pinetree Garden and the small gardens nearby were entirely redesigned, the pavilion at the end of the Maintenon Carriageway, dating back to François I, was demoli-

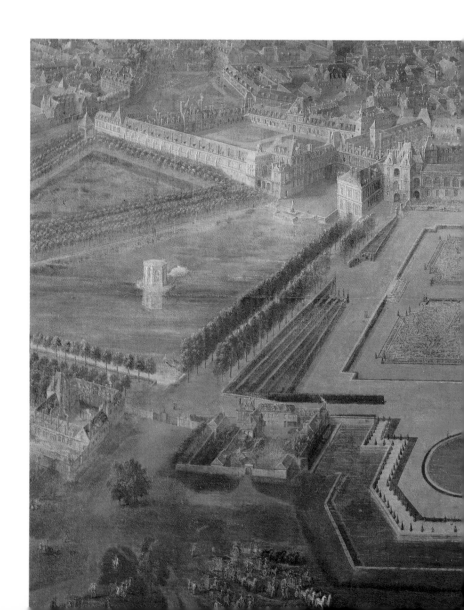

shed and the king's apartment was renovated (the bedchamber and cabinet were enlarged, an antechamber was made between this cabinet and the François I gallery).

Even though the reign of Louis XIV left no deep imprint on Fontainebleau, it was a very different matter with Louis XV (fig. 22). The requirements of life at court, changes in taste, not to mention the ideas of the king and his principal architect, provoked modifications that resulted in some regrettable destruction. Robert de Cotte first proposed to enclose the Fountain Courtyard

22.
Maurice-Quentin de la Tour, *Louis XV* (Paris, Musée du Louvre).

21.
Pierre-Denis Martin le Jeune, the château and gardens of Fontainebleau after the changes made in 1713 (Fontainebleau, Musée national du château).

(fig. 23) but his project was abandoned. With a view to providing more lodgings for the courtiers, a new wing was built in the Princes Courtyard (1737-1738). It was then decided to demolish the remarkable Ulysses Gallery and to replace it by the present Louis XV Wing; only the east portion and the central pavilion were built between 1738 and 1741, and work was not resumed until 1773-

1774. The Gabriels, father and son, had intended this operation to be the starting point of an almost complete remodelling of the château, affecting the whole of the White Horse Courtyard (fig. 24) and part of the Fountain Courtyard. However Ange-Jacques Gabriel only succeeded later in building the Large Pavilion in place of the Stove Pavilion of François I (1750-1754). Furthermore, in the course of the reign, the fronts of the royal apartments on the Diana Garden side were rebuilt during alterations indoors. At Fontainebleau as elsewhere, Louis XV particularly enjoyed modifying the arrangement and the decoration of his apartments. In 1725, the Jacquet chimneypiece was dismantled when a theatre was built in the Fine Chimney Wing (fig. 25). In 1736-1737, the king ordered the installation on the ground floor of some small apartments, which he thereafter enlarged and transformed continuously until his death (all these arrangements, which included finally an antechamber for buffets, a dining-room, a large reception room, another cabinet, a library, a baths apartment and kitchens, have

23.
Design to enclose the Fountain Courtyard
on the side of the pond, by the architect Robert de Cotte,
1729 (not carried out), watercolour drawing
(Paris, Bibliothèque nationale).
Left, the east end of the Ulysses Gallery, the billiardroom
and the roof of the Stove Pavilion are visible.

24.
Design to replace the wing at the entrance
to the White Horse Courtyard,
by the architect Ange-Jacques Gabriel, 1773
(not carried out), watercolour drawing
(Paris, Archives nationales).

25.
The theatre built by the architect Robert de Cotte
in 1724-1725, elevation, watercolour drawing
(Paris, Bibliothèque nationale).

25

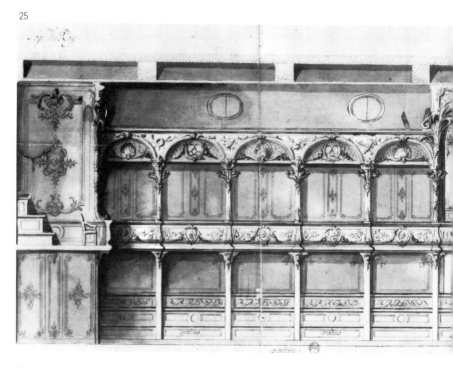

23

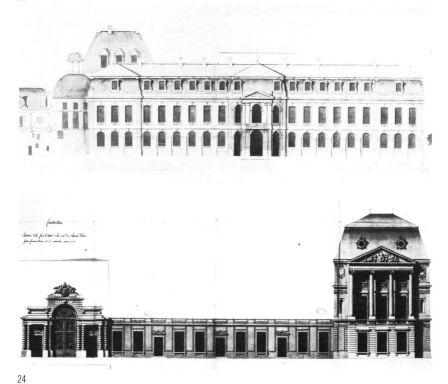

24

now completely disappeared). In 1737, in the king's state apartment on the first floor, a retreat in *rocaille* style replaced the antechamber of 1714; a new staircase was made in Madame d'Etampes' bedroom (1748-1749); the king's antechamber and dining-room (Saint Louis Chamber) were deprived of their 16th- to 17th-century decoration (1757); in the second antechamber (or Theagenes Chamber), the Henri-IV decoration was impaired when four large doors were pierced in the walls (1757); the king's bedchamber was enlarged and renovated, part of the 17th-century decor being kept and a fine design added "in antique taste" (1752-1754); the Council Chamber was given an entirely new painted ornamentation (1751-1753) and then enlarged to form a hemicycle (1772-1773). In the queen's apartment, alterations were made above all to her private rooms on the first floor and on the mezzanine (1737, 1746-1747, 1752) and to her bedchamber (1746-1747). In order to house her domestic staff, the Clorinda Room was demolished and a new staircase was made for her (1768). In the princes' and princesses' quarters, many changes took place; Gabriel built a hermitage near the château for Madame de Pompadour.

26.
Joseph-Siffred Duplessis,
Louis XVI
(Versailles, Musée national du château).

During the reign of Louis XVI (fig. 26), the main transformations in the château also concerned the king's and the queen's apartments. The king's private cabinet was restored in 1776, a Turkish boudoir (fig. 27) was decorated for Marie-Antoinette in 1777 by the Rousseau brothers, a billiard-room was installed outside near the king's private apartments in 1778. Owing to budgetary restrictions caused by the American War of Independence, work did not start again until 1783 with, notably, the installation of Mesdames, Louis XVI's aunts, in the new Princes Wing (Louis XV Wing). In 1784, some work continued in the private apartments, but by 1785, owing to the incoherent layout coupled with problems of water infiltration beneath the terrace of the François I Gallery, the king, the *Directeur Général des Bâtiments*, d'Angiviller, and the architect of the château, Potain, had to reconsider the whole issue. They decided to knock down the adventitious constructions in the Diana Garden, to demolish the rooms below the terrace and to raise a wing alongside the François I Gallery that would suit perfectly the needs of the sovereign: a private apartment on the first floor and a small one on the ground floor. Work progressed rapidly in 1785-1786 and a simple decoration was chosen, so that the king was able to benefit from these new installations during his annual sojourn in 1786. At the same time, the gamesroom and the retreat in the

27.
Turkish boudoir,
detail of the wood panelling.

queen's apartments were remarkably embellished in arabesque style, under the supervision of Potain's son-in-law, the architect Pierre Rousseau (fig. 28). These new decorations in the fashion of the day were continued the following year, in 1787, with alterations to the doors in the sovereign's bedchamber. In the private dining-room, four large pictures by Hubert Robert were hung, depicting *The Antiquities of Languedoc* (fig. 29).

During the Revolution, the château was damaged but not irreparably. Though a few portraits were burnt, certain emblems destroyed and casement windows and mirrors removed, little actual destruction took place. The château housed first the Ecole centrale of the Seine-et-Marne Département in 1796 and then, in 1803, the Ecole spéciale militaire, founded by Bonaparte. These occupations helped save the building from destruction.

29

29.
Hubert Robert. *Antique Monuments at Orange and St. Rémy de Provence*, 1787 (Paris, Musée du Louvre).

28.
Design probably intended for the decor of the Queen's bedchamber, attributed to the architect Pierre Rousseau (not carried out), watercolour drawing, 1786 (Fontainebleau, Musée national du château).

28

30.
Robert Lefèvre. *Napoléon I.*
(Versailles, Musée national
du château).

When Napoléon (fig. 30) became Emperor, a new era opened in the history of the château. Fontainebleau again became the residence of the sovereign (fig. 31). Napoléon loved this palace steeped in history and did his best to restore it. In fact, though his achievements were considerable in terms of refurbishing the apartments that had been stripped during the Revolution, his contribution to the architecture (fig. 32) and to the interior decoration was more modest. His most spectacular operation was the demoli-

31

tion in 1808 – when the Ecole spéciale militaire was transferred to Saint Cyr – of the François I wing looking on to Ferrara Place, and its replacement by wrought-iron railings (completed in 1810). The fall of the Empire however prevented the realisation of a subsidiary project that involved clearing the approaches to the château and creating a semicircular parade-ground with converging avenues. Inside, the most notable embellishments concerned the Diana Gallery – where the architect Hurtault got rid of the damaged

Henri-IV decor and in 1810 started on an overall restoration (still unfinished in 1814) – and Napoléon's private apartment – where, in 1811, Moench adorned the bedchamber and small bedroom with paintings in gilt grisaille. The upper Saint Saturnin Chapel was turned into a library (1806). Two gardens were replanted in the English manner, the Diana Garden and the former Pinetree Garden, henceforth called the English Garden. The Diana (fig. 33) and Perseus Fountains were restored.

32

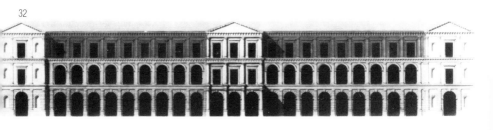

33

31.
Jean-Joseph-Xavier Bidault and Louis-Léopold Boilly.
Napoléon and Marie-Louise boating on the Pond.
(Paris, Musée Marmottan).

32.
Design to replace the Horseshoe Staircase Wing,
attributed to the architect Maximilien-Joseph Hurtault,
c. 1810 (not carried out), drawing (Paris, Archives nationales).

33.
The Diana Garden in 1842.
Plate from the Sèvres porcelain historic service of Fontainebleau painted by Jules André (Fontainebleau, Musée national du château).
The fountain reconstituted by Napoléon can be seen,
as well as the small iron staircase in the background which led straight down from the first floor to the garden.

35.
Franz-Xaver
Winterhalter.
Louis-Philippe
(Versailles, Musée
national du château).

During the Restoration period (1815 to 1830), the Diana Gallery was completed (fig. 34) and important repairs were made in the Trinity Chapel, but it was not until the reign of Louis-Philippe (fig. 35) that a real revival of the royal residence took place. The new king – with a passion for history and art and anxious to preserve the heritage of the past – wanted to carry out a veritable renovation. His intention was not really to undertake a faithful restoration, but rather to enhance the existing decoration by completing or rearranging it, if need be. This huge entreprise was often a work of creation (more or less original), inspired by past styles.

As far as the main fabric of the building was concerned, nothing important was done. The most regrettable event was the demolition of the former orangery (set on fire in 1789) and that of the nearby Roe Gallery; elsewhere alterations consisted mainly in advancing the façades, thought necessary to make it easier to circulate within the château (Princes Courtyard, the wing overlooking the terrace of the White Horse Courtyard, the passage between the guardroom and the François I Gallery). The architect Dubreuil faithfully reproduced the former appearance of these façades.

In the apartments, priority was given above all to renovating the Renaissance rooms and the state apartments overlooking the Oval Courtyard. New wood panelling and a new floor were installed in the ballroom, then called the Henri II Gallery, while the mural paintings were freshened up by Alaux (1835-1836); the decoration of the King's Staircase was renovated and completed by the painter Abel de Pujol (1835-1836) and that of the Golden Gate by Picot (1835). Refurbishment of the François I Gallery did not start until the end of the reign (1847). In the state apartments, several reception rooms were embellished in Renaissance style: wall hangings and painted wood panels in the guardroom and the adjoining rotunda; fireplaces composed of pieces of existing sculptures, in the same

24

room and in the second Saint Louis Chamber; a mantlepiece in Sèvres porcelain after models by Klagmann in the François I Chamber (unfortunateley removed in 1964); a coffered ceiling in the Tapestry Chamber. There was also a revival of the Louis-XIV style, evident in the Maintenon apartment,

34.
The Diana Gallery in 1839,
watercolour by Thomas Allom
(Fontainebleau, Musée
national du château).
The great vase, known as the Phidias vase,
in Sèvres biscuit,
was placed here in 1838.

on the ceilings of the two Saint Louis Chambers and of the Queen's Staircase.

Another of the king's main preoccupations was the rehabilitation of disfigured sites: the lower Chapel of Saint Saturnin became once again a place of worship (stained-glass windows made at Sèvres from cartoons by Princesse Marie, the king's daughter, and by Emile Wattier) (fig. 36); the ground floor beneath the ballroom was transformed into a large waiting room in Renaissance style, called the Louis-Philippe Chamber (today the Columns Gallery) (fig. 37); the small rooms for the queen's domestic staff near the Diana Gallery made way for a room adorned with Louis-XV panelling; the Duc d'Orléans' antechamber lost its mezzanine and was given a ceiling in carton pierre; the ground floor of the keep, below the

Saint Louis Chamber, was transformed by association of ideas into a vaulted vestibule in Gothic style (fig. 38) and adorned with plaster statues of kings. In several places the king also strove to enhance the mural decoration by placing in the wood panels ancient pictures recuperated elsewhere. This was the case in the Saint Louis Chambers, in the apartment of the young princes (today's Hunts Apartment on the first floor), in the Queen's Staircase, in the small room between the guardroom and the theatre, as well as in the new Fresco Gallery behind the prince royal's apartment. In 1844, a small room of painted glass from Louis XVI's period was brought to Fontainebleau from the Paris mansion formerly the *Garde-meuble de la Couronne* and installed near the king's bathroom (removed in 1964).

37

36

38

36.
Lower Saint Saturnin Chapel,
stained glass in the apse
dedicated to Saint Philip,
Saint Saturnin and Saint Amelia,
Manufacture de Sèvres, 1834-1836.

37.
The Columns Gallery,
lithograph by Philippe Benoist,
at the time of Louis-Philippe.

38.
The Saint Louis
Vestibule, lithograph,
at the time
of Louis-Philippe.

39.
Franz-Xaver
Winterhalter.
Napoléon III
(Compiègne, Musée
national du château).

The period of the Second Republic was not a dormant one at Fontainebleau. Restoration work was carried out in the François I Gallery and the Horseshoe Staircase Pavilion was consolidated. It is certain that the election of Prince Louis-Napoléon as head of state inevitably benefited Fontainebleau. Soon afterwards, with the restoration of the Empire, it regained considerable importance. Napoléon III (fig. 39), like Louis-Philippe, took a great interest in the renovation of the château, pursuing it without interruption. A good deal of work was carried out in the Trinity Chapel (1854-1860), the François I Gallery (completed in 1861), the ballroom of the former apartment of the Pope, the private apartments, the Hunts Apartments and the Princes Courtyard. The

most interesting enterprise was the renovation of the Stags Gallery, where the apartments installed by Napoléon I were removed and the Henri-IV decoration restored (1860-1868). Mention must be made of the decoration for the new theatre (1854) (fig. 40) designed by the architect Lefuel in the Louis-XVI style, two drawing rooms on the ground floor of the Large Pavilion (*Gros Pavillon*) in Chinese fashion (1863, 1868) (fig. 41), the Great Events Gallery and the Philippe-Auguste Staircase with stucco work.

The fall of the Second Empire put an end to these embellishments. The campanila of Saint Saturnin Chapel was reconstituted by the architect Boitte in 1882, and the upper parts of the Fine Chimney Wing, burnt in 1856, were reconstructed in 1927-1931, thanks to the Rockefeller Foundation. It was not until the middle of the 20th century that a new overall restoration project was formulated and undertaken. The 1964-1968 Act providing the framework for the government Programme for Cultural Affairs, instigated by André Malraux, permitted the consolidation of the main fabric of the buildings, the uncovering of the frescoes of the great Renaissance masters which

40.
Theatre in the Louis XV Wing, stereoscopic view at the time of the Second Empire.

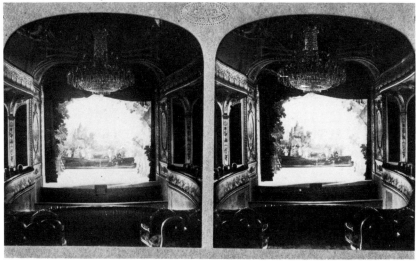

had been painted over in the 19th century, together with the renovation of the sovereigns' state apartments looking on to the Diana Garden.

Since then, other important operations have been carried out in the framework of the 1978-1982 Programme Act for Museums: restoration of the Golden Gate Pavilion and the Maintenon apartment (1979-1983), as well as the creation, in the Louis XV Wing, of a great museum devoted to Napoléon I and his family (1979-1986). Restoration work continued on the Trinity Chapel. Since 1983, work has been done to the Chinese Museum, the Pope's apartment and the Emperor's private apartment.

41.
"The Empress's Chinese Museum", from *Le Monde illustré*, 4 July 1863.

42.
Saint Thomas Becket
consecrating a Church,
detail of a stained glass,
c. 1207-1215
(Sens, Cathedral).

43.
Head of the gisant statue
of Philippe le Bel,
marble (Saint-Denis,
Cathedral).

44.
François Clouet,
François II, drawing
(Paris, Bibiothèque
nationale).

43

Historical events *

1169		Consecration by Saint Thomas Becket, Archbishop of Canterbury, during his exile in France, of the chapel of the Château de Fontainebleau, dedicated to the Virgin Mary and Saint Saturnin (fig. 42).
1268		Birth of Philippe (later King Philippe IV le Bel), son of Prince Philippe and of Isabella of Aragon and grandson of Saint Louis.
1314	29 November	Death of Philippe IV le Bel (fig. 43).
1323		Visit of Isabelle de France, Queen of England, to her brother Charles IV le Bel.
1332	January	Signing of the marriage settlement between Jean de France (later Jean II le Bon) and Bonne of Bohemia.
1536	4-27 December	Visit of King James V of Scotland (before his marriage in Paris on 1st January 1537 to Madeleine, daughter of François I, in Paris).
1539	24-30 December	Visit of the Emperor Charles V.
1544	19 January	Birth of François (later François II), son of the Dauphin Henri and of Catherine de Médicis (fig. 44).
1544	10 February	Baptism of this Prince.
1546	2 April	Birth of Élisabeth (later Queen of Spain), eldest daughter of the Dauphin Henri and of Catherine de Médicis.
1547	12 November	Birth of Claude (later Duchesse de Lorraine), second daughter of Henri II and Catherine de Médicis.
1551	19 September	Birth of Edouard-Alexandre (later Henri III), fourth son of Henri II and Catherine de Médicis.
1555	18 March	Birth of Hercule (later François, Duc d'Anjou), fifth son of Henri II and Catherine de Médicis.
1556	24 June	Birth of Jeanne and Victoire, fourth and fifth daughers of Henri II and Catherine de Médicis.
1560	21-31 August	Assemblée des Notables to pacify the religious disturbances. The decision was taken to convoke the Etats Généraux.
1599	14-21 December	Reception of Charles-Emmanuel, Duke of Savoy.
1600	4 May	Debate in the presence of Henri IV between Monseigneur du Perron, Bishop of Évreux, and the Protestant theologian Duplessis-Mornay, on proposals put forward by the latter in his *Traité de l'Eucharistie*.
1601	12 June	Wedding of Concini and Leonora Dori Galigaï in the King's Chapel.
1601	27 September	Birth of the Dauphin (later Louis XIII), son of Henri IV and Marie de Médicis.

* Only a very few of the receptions given for ambassadors are mentioned.

45

1602	14 June	Arrest of the Maréchal de Biron and the Comte d'Auvergne on a charge of treason (the former was beheaded in Paris on 29 July).
1602	22 November	Birth of Élisabeth (later Queen of Spain), daughter of Henri IV and Marie de Médicis.
1606	14 September	Baptism of the Dauphin and his sisters Élisabeth and Chrétienne in the Oval Courtyard (fig. 45).
1608	25 April	Birth of the Duc d'Anjou (later Gaston, Duc d'Orléans), third son of Henri IV and Marie de Médicis.
1609	7 July	Wedding of César, Duc de Vendôme, legitimised son of the King and of Gabrielle d'Estrées, and Henriette de Lorraine, daughter of the Duc de Mercoeur.
1626	4 May	Arrest of Maréchal d'Ornano.
1629	16 September	Ratification of the peace treaty between France and England.
1633	14-15 May	Promotion of 49 knights of the Ordre du Saint-Esprit (fig. 46).
1645	25 September	Signing in the King's bedchamber of the marriage settlement between Ladislas IV, King of Poland, and Marie de Gonzague.
1646	19-23 August	Reception of Henriette-Marie de France, Queen of England, and her son the Prince of Wales, future Charles II.
1656	4-6 September	First visit of Queen Christina of Sweden (fig. 47).

46

47

45.
The Christening of Louis XIII
and his Sisters
in the Oval Courtyard,
engraving by Léonard Gaultier.

46.
Procession of the Knights
of the Saint-Esprit
in the Fountain Courtyard,
Sunday, 15 May 1633,
engraving by Abraham Bosse.

47.
Sébastien Bourdon.
Christina of Sweden, drawing
(Paris, Musée du Louvre).

48.
Audience of the Cardinal Legate
Chigi in the King's Bedchamber,
Gobelins tapestry
(set of *The History of the King*)
from a drawing by Lebrun
(Versailles, Musée national
du château).

1657	10 November	Assassination in the Stags Gallery of Monaldeschi, Master of the Horse to Queen Christina of Sweden, commanded by the Queen herself. (The Queen stayed at Fontainebleau from 10 October 1657 to 23 February 1658).
1661	17 August	Louis XIV leaves Fontainebleau to attend the famous festivities at the Château de Vaux organised in his honour by Fouquet. Furious at the lavish display of luxury at the Château, the King thereupon decides to have his Surintendant des finances imprisoned.
1661	1 November	Birth of the Dauphin Louis, son of Louis XIV and Marie-Thérèse d'Autriche.
1664	25 June to the beginning of August	The Court of Justice in charge of the trial of Fouquet holds session in the Chancellory at Fontainebleau.

1664	29 July	Cardinal Chigi, legate to Pope Alexander VII, received in audience. He came to present the Pope's apologies following the clash in Rome in 1662 between the Corsican Papal Guards and servants of the French Ambassador (fig. 48).
1679	31 August	Marriage by proxy in the Trinity Chapel of Charles II, King of Spain and Marie-Louise d'Orléans, known as Mademoiselle, daughter of Monsieur and of Henrietta of England.
1679	2 September	Treaty between France and Sweden on the one hand, and Denmark and the Duke of Holstein-Gottorp on the other.
1685	17 October	Revocation of the Edict of Nantes by the Edict of Fontainebleau.
1685	9 November	Death of Louis-Armand de Bourbon, Prince de Conti, Louis XIV's son-in-law.

1686	11 December	Death of Louis de Bourbon, Prince de Condé, called Monsieur le Prince (le Grand Condé), at the age of 65 (fig. 49).	
1690	11-18 October	First visit of the exiled King of England, James II and his wife Mary of Modena (until 1700 they returned to stay in Fontainebleau every year, while Louis XIV was in residence there).	
1696	5 November	Arrival of Marie-Adélaïde de Savoie, future Duchesse de Bourgogne.	
1698	13 October	Marriage by proxy of Léopold, Duc de Lorraine and Élisabeth-Charlotte d'Orléans, known as Mademoiselle, daughter of Monsieur and Élisabeth-Charlotte, Princesse Palatine.	

49.
Antoine Coysevox.
Le Grand Condé,
bronze (Paris,
Musée du
Louvre).

1700	9-11 November	Louis XIV holds several council meetings in Madame de Maintenon's apartment and decides to accept the King of Spain's will making the Duc d'Anjou his heir.
1712	21-24 August	Lord Bolingbroke is sent to Fontainebleau by Queen Anne for the peace negociations between France and England to end the War of the Spanish Succession.
1714	26 September	Reception of Frederick-Augustus, Elector of Saxony, under the name of Comte de Lusace (future King Augustus III of Poland).
1717	30-31 May	The Tsar Peter the Great visits Fontainebleau.
1725	5 September	Wedding of Louis XV and Marie Leszczynska, Princess of Poland (fig. 50).
1743	27 October	Secret treaty of alliance between France and Spain.
1752	18 October	First performance of the *Devin du Village* by Jean-Jacques Rousseau (fig. 51).

50. *Wedding of Louis XV in the Trinity Chapel*, engraving by an unknown artist.

1765	20 December	Death of the Dauphin Louis, only son of Louis XV, aged 36 (fig. 52).
1768	24-27 October and 2-5 November	King Christian VII of Denmark stays at Fontainebleau.
1771	12 May	Arrival of Marie-Joséphine-Louise de Savoie, future Comtesse de Provence.
1773	14 November	Arrival of Marie-Thérèse de Savoie, sister of the Comtesse de Provence and future Comtesse d'Artois.
1786	10 November	Ratification of the Trade Treaty between France and England.
1803 (Year XI)	28 January (8 Pluviôse)	Decree providing for the establishment of the Ecole spéciale militaire at Fontainebleau.
1804	25-28 November	First visit of Pope Pius VII to Fontainebleau (fig. 53).
1807	10 October	Treaty fixing the frontiers between Austria and the Kingdom of Italy.

51.
Frontispiece to the edition of the score for
Le Devin du village

52.
Alexandre Roslin.
Louis de France, the Dauphin.
(Versailles, Musée national du château).

53.
Louis David (studio of).
Pope Pius VII
(Fontainebleau, Musée national du château).

54.
Signature of the Concordate,
engraving by Giovanni Petrini.

54b.
The Concordate of Fontainebleau,
last page bearing the signatures
of the Pope and the Emperor
(Paris, Archives du ministère
des Affaires étrangères).

1807	15 October	Treaty of alliance between France and Denmark.
1807	27 October	Secret treaty between France and Spain concerning Portugal.
1808	23 May to beginning of June	King Charles IV of Spain and Queen Maria Luisa stay at Fontainebleau, accompanied by Godoy.
1808	30 June	Transfer of the Ecole spéciale militaire from Fontainebleau to Saint-Cyr.
1810	4 November	Baptism of Prince Louis-Charles-Napoléon (future Napoléon III) in the chapel at the Château with twenty-four children of dignitaries and generals.
1812	19 June	Arrival of Pope Pius VII at Fontainebleau, where he will remain for nineteen months. Napoléon places him under house arrest.
1813	25 January	Concordate of Fontainebleau (fig. 54 and 54b).
1814	23 January	Departure of Pope Pius VII.
1814	4 April	Conditional abdication of Napoléon.
1814	6 April	Unconditional abdication of Napoléon.
1814	Night of 12/13 April	Napoléon attempts to commit suicide.
1814	20 April	Napoléon departs for the Island of Elba. He takes leave of the Imperial Guard (fig. 55).

55. Antoine Montfort, after Horace Vernet. *Napoléon taking leave of the Imperial Guard in the White Horse Courtyard* (Versailles, Musée national du château).

56.
Civil wedding ceremony of Ferdinand-Philippe,
Duc d'Orléans, son of Louis-Philippe with Princess Helen
von Mecklenburg-Schwerin in the ballroom.
Plaque on a commemorative casket in Sèvres porcelain
painted by Jean-Charles Develly
(Fontainebleau, Musée national du château).

1815	20 March	Napoléon makes a brief stop at Fontainebleau on his return from Elba.
1816	15 June	Arrival of the Duchesse de Berry, Marie-Caroline de Bourbon-Sicile.
1837	30 May	Wedding of Ferdinand-Philippe, Duc d'Orléans, son of Louis-Philippe, and Helen of Mecklenburg-Schwerin (fig. 56).
1840	20-21 November	Visit of the ex-Queen of Spain, Maria Cristina.
1846	16 April	Attempt on the life of Louis-Philippe in the park of the Château de Fontainebleau, perpetrated by Pierre Lecomte, former forest warden.
1846	15-16 December	Visit of the Bey of Tunis Sidi Achmet.
1856	15-16 December	Visit of the Prince Royal of Prussia (future Kaiser Wilhelm I).
1857	17-24 May	Visit of Maximilian II, King of Bavaria.
1861	27 June	Reception of the Siamese ambassadors (fig. 57).
1870	17 September	Arrival of the Prussians.
1871	6-18 March	Prince Frederick Charles of Prussia and his chiefs of staff occupy the Château.
1871	23 March	Departure of the Prussian troops.
1871	November	The Ecole d'Application de l'Artillerie et du Génie (Artillery and Engineer Corps), formerly in Metz, is installed in the Château.
1891	17 August	King Alexander Ist of Serbia is received by Sadi Carnot, President of the Republic.

57

1892	9 September	King George I of Greece is received by Sadi Carnot.
1895	21 September	The President Félix Faure holds a reception for the King of the Belgians, Léopold II.
1913	8 May	Raymond Poincaré receives Alfonso XIII, King of Spain.
1914	10 July	The former Empress Eugénie visits the Château.
1921	26 June	Inauguration of the American Conservatory.
1923	25 June	Inauguration of the American School of Fine Arts.
1940	16 June	Entry of the German army, commanded by General Ruoff (the Château is occupied by the German army until 10 November 1940, then from 15 May to late October 1941).
1946	6 July to 10 September	Franco-Vietnamese Conference presided over by Max André and Pham-Van-Dong (fig. 58).
1948	5 October	Creation of the International Union for the Protection of Nature.
1949	January	Part of the Château serves as headquarters for the Centre-Europe Command of the Allied Forces (NATO).
1966	July	Departure of the Centre-Europe headquarters.
1984	25-26 June	Meeting of the Council of the heads of state and government of the European Economic Community, presided over by M. François Mitterrand, President of the Republic.
1986	10 June	Inauguration of the Musée Napoléon Ier.

58

57.
Jean-Léon Gérôme.
Napoléon III receiving the Siamese Ambassadors in the Ballroom
(Versailles, Musée national du château).

58.
Inaugural session of the Franco-Vietnamese Conference in the Columns Gallery: Max André standing and M. Pham-Van-Dong facing him.

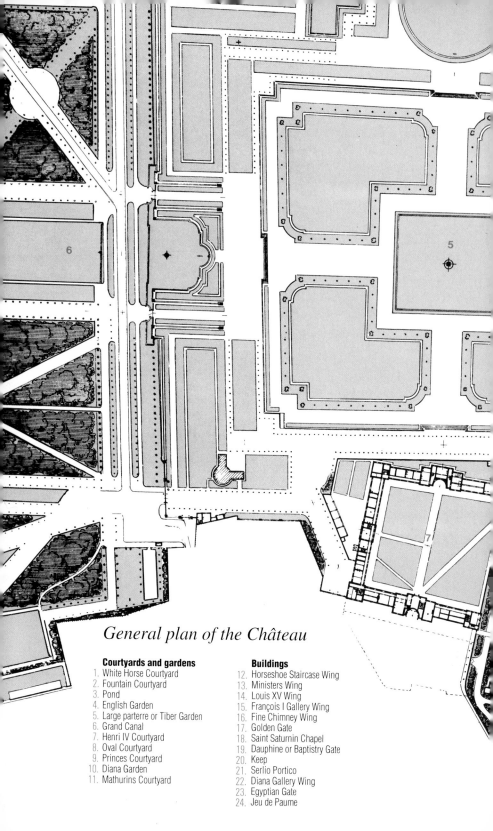

General plan of the Château

Courtyards and gardens
1. White Horse Courtyard
2. Fountain Courtyard
3. Pond
4. English Garden
5. Large parterre or Tiber Garden
6. Grand Canal
7. Henri IV Courtyard
8. Oval Courtyard
9. Princes Courtyard
10. Diana Garden
11. Mathurins Courtyard

Buildings
12. Horseshoe Staircase Wing
13. Ministers Wing
14. Louis XV Wing
15. François I Gallery Wing
16. Fine Chimney Wing
17. Golden Gate
18. Saint Saturnin Chapel
19. Dauphine or Baptistry Gate
20. Keep
21. Serlio Portico
22. Diana Gallery Wing
23. Egyptian Gate
24. Jeu de Paume

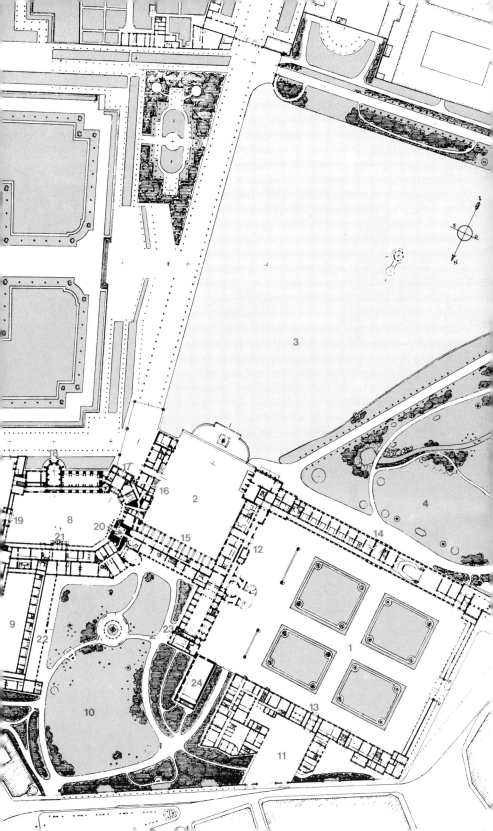

59.
The Horseshoe Staircase Wing.

60.
The Ministers Wing.

59

60

Buildings, courtyards and gardens

The White Horse Courtyard (fig. 59)

This courtyard is enclosed by high iron railings (1809-1810), the central part lavishly adorned with Napoleonic ensigns. The two gilt lead eagles, removed in 1814, were ceremoniously put back on 1 April 1848, removed again in 1870 and reinstalled in January 1911. The buildings surrounding the White Horse Courtyard are very varied in style; the low wing on the left (c. 1530 in the reign of François I), called the Ministers Wing (*Aile des Ministres*) (fig. 60), is built of brick and mortar rubble on sandstone foundations, on either side of a central pavilion. Though the apertures have changed in the course of time, it is still evident that originally there were low windows and doors surmounted by pediments (some of which have been rediscovered) at regular intervals on each side of the central pavilion in nine bays of different widths, partitioned by pilasters. In the roofs the dormer windows are decorated with pilasters and curved pediments (all rebuilt in 1878 in accordance with 16th-century prints). The pavilion

62

63   61

has one large dormer window with three bays, the middle one between two niches, with a narrower top decorated with a salamander, framed in scrollwork and surmounted by a pediment. This dormer window was also rebuilt in 1878 (in the 16th century there were some salamander medallions where the two lateral windows on the first floor of the pavilion on the courtyard side are now placed). The chimneys on this pavilion bear pilasters and the letter F for François I. The building comes to an abrupt stop with the railings at the entrance to the Diana Garden. This last part is thought to have been demolished after the moat was made in 1565, though probably not immediately afterwards. Beyond the railings is the royal tennis court (*jeu de paume*), no longer decorated as it had been in Henri IV's day, but as it was reconstructed in 1732 (after having caught fire in 1702).

The wing on the far side of the courtyard, famous for the horseshoe stairs (1632-1634) (fig. 61 and 62) and strongly punctuated by five pavilions, seems to be a mixture of styles and shapes. The parts dating from the reign of François I are faced with sandstone and mortar rubble, and ornamented with pilasters and dormer windows with a triangular pediment: from left to right, the Arms Pavilion (*Pavillon des Armes*), the Clock Tower (*Tour de l'Horloge*), the second pavilion known as the Organ Pavilion (*Pavillon des Orgues*) and the three neighbouring bays, then beyond the central pavilion there is the fourth pavilion, today wrongly called the Stove Pavilion (*Pavillon des Poêles*), part of the outer walls of which is curiously faced with dressed stone. (The small building between the Clock Tower and the Organ Pavilion built in 1664, also in sandstone, heightened in Louis XV's time and

61.
The Horseshoe Staircase: in the background, the Jeu de Paume, the Aumôniers Pavilion, the Clock Tower and the Organ Pavilion.

62.
Detail of the Horseshoe Staircase: a caduceus.

63.
Door on the first floor of the central pavilion of the Horseshoe Staircase Wing.

64.
The intermediary pavilion between the Large Pavilion and the Louis XV Wing, façade overlooking the White Horse Courtyard.

64

later transformed in the reign of Charles X by introducing a row of semicircular windows above, should be considered apart.) The rest of the wing has ashlar walls in a classical Renaissance style, with, on the ground floor, arches with rusticated pilasters, surmounted on the first floor by doric pilasters and in the roof, by dormer windows with a broken curved pediment adorned with a mascaron at the sides. These changes started with the reconstruction by Henri II and Charles IX of the wing called the Queen Mothers' Wing (*Aile des Reines Mères*) and the creation of a central pavilion (1558-1565). A complete overhaul of the building was then planned but never finished, though work was undertaken in the part situated south of the grand staircase, first by Henri IV and Louis XIII (arcades on the ground floor, niches), then by Louis XV (upper parts of the pavilion on the far right,

originally in sandstone too) and finally by Louis-Philippe (the terrace being demolished to make way for the Plates Gallery (*Galerie des Assiettes*). Hence this composite look, increased by the absence of dormer windows on the chapel side. The elaborate carving on the centre door at the top of the steps dates back to the reign of Louis XIII. The bust of François I, copied from the statue of the King praying at Saint Denis, was placed in a niche in the reign of Louis-Philippe (fig. 63).

The south side of the courtyard is very different in aspect. It begins with a stone pavilion (1739) where Jacques Gabriel adopted the Renaissance layout, though he innovated in the ground-floor bays and the attic, introducing in particular the depressed arches adorned with shell and floral keystones (fig.64). Then comes the somewhat monotonous Louis XV wing (1739-1740 and 1773-1774) in brick and stone to harmonise with the adjacent low buildings

65

(fig. 65 and 66). The height of this building had already spoilt the proportions of the court-yard, before this even more regrettable modi-fication occurred, when the wing looking on to the square was demolished and replaced by the present iron railings (1808-1810). Near the rai-lings the corner pavilion, heavily restored, which ended the two wings, still remains and it is in the same style as its pendant. On the garden side, it houses the famous Pinetree Grotto (*Grotte des Pins*) (fig. 67) with its great rustic atlantes. The interior decoration which had completely disappeared is now being reconstituted.

The four great squares in the courtyard were covered with grass lawns in 1868. The

66

67

two open balustrades dating from 1843 have taken the place of the old west parapet of the 16th-century moat which crossed the courtyard (this moat seems to have been filled in when in 1803 the Ecole spéciale militaire was created). The two pedestals near the staircase are each garnished with a bronze mask cast in 1609 which had once served as a fountain.

65.
The Louis XV Wing,
façade overlooking the English garden.

66.
Central pavilion of the Louis XV Wing,
façade overlooking the White Horse Courtyard.

67.
The Pinetree garden Grotto,
façade overlooking the English garden.

The Fountain Courtyard, the Pond and the English Garden (fig. 68)

On entering the Fountain Courtyard (*Cour de la Fontaine*) we receive on the contrary an impression of unity created by the the same stone material employed everywhere and a similarity of architectural forms (with the exception of the Large Pavilion close to the pond). The Queen Mothers' Wing (1558-1565) (fig. 69), has replaced a low wing linking the François I Gallery to the Stove Pavilion. After this came the Fine Chimney Wing (*Aile de la Belle Cheminée*) (fig. 70) (*c.* 1565-1570), parallel to it, which encompassed a construction erected by François I. This building was conceived in the truly grand manner. With its great roofs, the noble arrangement of its two straight flights of steps, the fine mouldings, it is among the most remarkable examples of French 16th-century architecture, a synthesis of French and Italian art which mingles the ideas of Serlio and Delorme. Indeed Primaticcio may well have found inspiration in the great accomplishments of Bramante at the Vatican or of Michelangelo

at the Capitol, when he made the flights of steps which mount in diverging directions (the original aspect of the façade was somewhat altered when bays were opened up on the ground floor on the left). The wing at the far end of the courtyard (fig. 71) which houses the François I Gallery, the oldest one and originally in sandstone and mortar, has been faced with ashlar like the Queen Mothers' Wing. The number of dormer windows was unfortunately doubled in Louis-Philippe's time. The terraced gallery bordering it, which dates from Henri IV, copies the system of double pilasters and niches on the ground floor of the corner pavilions of the Fine Chimney Wing, but the niches have been replaced since the 18th century by bays intended to give more light to the King's private apartments. Finally, the elevation of the *Gros Pavillon* (fig. 72), which replaced in 1750 the former Stove Pavilion, was imposed by the adjoining Queen Mothers' Wing. Its decoration is inspired by the art of Versailles, with a rusticated ground floor, the projecting part of the first floor adorned with columns, an attic, and a balustrade with trophies and flame ornaments (these disappeared in the early 19th century).

68. The pond, the Pond Pavilion and the buildings round the Fountain Courtyard.

69.
The Queen Mothers' Wing
and the Large Pavilion,
façade overlooking the
Fountain Courtyard.

70.
The Fine Chimney Wing,
façade overlooking
the Fountain Courtyard.

71.
The François I Gallery Wing,
façade overlooking the
Fountain Courtyard.

72.
The Large Pavilion
and the Ulysses Fountain.

The fountain which gave its name to the courtyard is seen today in the state it was in at the start of the 19th century : the pedestal and four bronze heads of Medusa (by Delafontaine) date from 1812, the statue of Ulysses by Louis Petitot (Salon of 1819) was set up in 1824. Beyond one can see the pond, frequently called the Carp Pond, a vast stretch of water fed by numerous springs. In the middle is an eight-sided pavilion built in 1662 in Louis XIV's day by Le Vau and restored by Napoléon I in 1807 (when unfortunately the roof was altered).

After passing by the Large Pavilion, we enter the English Garden (*Jardin anglais*) which was given its present form in the time of Napoléon I (fig. 73). A picturesque river runs through it. It is worth remarking among others, two bronze statues (entered in 1813) facing the Louis XV wing, the *Fighting Gladiateur*, after the "Borghese Gladiator"

(17th century), from an antique marble at the Musée du Louvre, signed Agasias of Ephesus, from the Hellenistic era (1st century B.C.), and the *Dying Gladiateur* (fig. 74) carved by Vinache in 1688 after a sculpture at the Capitol Museum in Rome, itself an antique replica of a bronze of the late 3rd century B.C., which was part of an ex-voto commissioned by King Attalus I of Pergamum to give thanks for his victories over the Galatians. Near the bottom of the garden, a basin marks the spot of the legendary *Fontaine Belle Eau* (which gave its name to Fontainebleau). Not far from the south bank of the pond (outside the estate, for the land has been conceded to the Ministry of Defence), the riding school built in Napoléon's time for the pupils of the Ecole spéciale militaire (1806-1808) is still standing (fig. 75). This building has remarkable structural work.

73

74   75

73.
The English garden.
74.
Joseph Vinache.
The Dying Gladiator,
from the Antique, bronze.
75.
The riding school.

Façades overlooking the large formal garden (fig. 76).

Returning to the Fountain Courtyard, we take the central passageway through the Fine Chimney Wing, the back façade of which reveals the original low construction work in sandstone with its single-chamfered windows (inside there is a corbel with the salamander motif). We are now standing in front of the Golden Gate (fig. 77), dating from 1528, which supplanted the entrance to the fortified castle. Built in sandstone and mortar rubble in the style of the Italian Renaissance, its most distinctive features are the loggias one above the other, reminiscent of the Castle of Urbino, and the ornamentation of pilasters and triangular pediments so characteristic of Fontainebleau at the time of François I. After a change in the orientation of the buildings imposed by the structure of

the medieval castle, appears the façade of the ballroom, the first floor of which, in dressed sandstone, is pierced by immense grooveless bays, revealing the original plan for an open loggia in the Italian manner. The ornamentation consists of small, rather incongruous pilasters, medallions decorated with royal monograms and emblems, keystones with mascarons and archaic-looking gargoyles. A balustrade crowns the edifice.

The apse of the Saint Saturnin chapels (fig. 78), built shortly before the ballroom, juts out on to the garden. Constructed in sandstone ashlar, it shows a rather elegant superposition of two architectural orders (pilasters and columns with composite capitals and a large entablature). The lantern of 1882 is a somewhat unsatisfactory pastiche. Next comes a building dating back to Henri IV, modelled on the ballroom wing and ending with a large angle pavilion of the

76

77   78

76.
Façades overlooking the great parterre: from left to right,
the Fine Chimney Wing,
the Golden Gate, the ballroom,
the upper and lower Saint Saturnin Chapels, the Tiber Pavilion.

77.
The Golden Gate.

78.
The apse of the upper
and lower Saint Saturnin Chapels.

55

79.
South wing on the
Offices Courtyard,
façades overlooking
the great parterre.

80.
Sully Pavilion.

81.
Mathieu Lespagnandel,
Female Sphinx, stone.

81

80

79

same period known as the Dauphins or Tiber Pavilion (*Pavillon des Dauphins* or *Pavillon du Tibre*), similar to the style of François I in the Keep Courtyard (many alterations were made to the apertures in the 19th century) with new elements added (scroll motifs on the gable windows, emblems of Henri IV on the capitals).

At the entrance to the former moat, two low brick and stone pavilions with large arcades were erected in Louis-Philippe's reign, when the wing of the Roe Gallery was demolished (see p. 24 above). Before approaching the gateway to the Oval Courtyard, it is worth walking along the south side of one wing of Henri IV's Offices Courtyard (fig. 79) (see below p. 61) to take a look at an isolated pavilion in brick and mortar rubble, dating from 1534 (fig. 80). This used to be the pendant of an identical pavilion, situated in the south-east corner of the garden, and it is called the Sully Pavilion,

although the famous Surintendant (Financial Secretary) probably never lived there. In the 17th century it was known as the Grand Chamberlain's Pavilion (*Pavillon du Grand Chambellan*), the other one being the Grand Master's Pavilion (*Pavillon du Grand Maître*).

The garden itself, long known as the Tiber Garden, owing to the bronze statue of the river placed there at the beginning of the 17th century, is in the French formal style and has still kept the design traced by Le Nôtre in 1660-1664. Unfortunately the clipped box-tree embroideries have disappeared. In the central fountain there is a large basin (1817) which has replaced the 17th-century rock-shaped fountain called the Boiling Pot. In 1988 a plastic moulding of the antique Tiber statue (Musée du Louvre) was put in the circular basin close to the forest, a reminder of the sculpture already mentioned, produced by the

82. The Cascades Basin, with the Sully Pavilion in the background.

Fontainebleau workshops which Le Nôtre had had transferred there in 1664, and which was destroyed during the Revolution. Eastwards, on the Grand Canal side, at the top of the sloping gardens, are four sandstone sphinxes by Mathieu Lespagnandel (1664) (fig. 81). The Cascade Fountain, partly ruined in 1723, was rebuilt during the Restoration. The sculptures were not installed until 1864 (with a few changes later) (fig. 82).

On top of the pillars of the iron railings (looking from left to right with your back to the canal), you can see eight marble statues or groups: *Zenobia, Queen of Armenia saved from drowning in the Araxes* by Marcellin (1859), *Aurelia Victorina, Princess of Gaul, nicknamed Mother of the Camps* by Daumas (1857) erected in 1866, *Amphitrite* by Cordier (1863) set up in 1866, *Adam* by Perraud (1853), *The Water Nymphs* by Desboeufs (1855), *Geneviève de Brabant* by Maindron (1859), *Bacchant and Satyr* by Crauk (Salon of 1859) placed in 1876 (?), *The Return of the Prodigal Son* by Gumery (1856). In the niches (still looking from left to right) there is a bronze group: *Indian Hunter coming Face to Face with a Boa* by Ottin (cast by V. Thiébaut, 1855), then eight marble statues: *Hebe* by Huguenin (1858), *The Muse of Inspiration* by Prouha (1858), *Chalcography* by Demesmay (1861), *Actæon* by Fulconis (1861), *Diana* or *Hunting* by Chabaud (1861), *Inspiration* by Chambard (1859), *Dido* by Ramus (1860), *Wisdom* by Lepère (1860) and finally another bronze group: *Zebra attacked by a Panther* by I. Bonheur (cast by E. Vittoz, 1854). In the middle of the basin there is *An Eagle preparing to defend its Prey* by Cain (cast by E. Vittoz) set up in 1866.

Beyond stretches the huge park with the Henri IV canal, approximately one thousand two hundred metres long.

83.
The Dauphine
or Baptistery Gateway
with the outer portal
in the Offices Courtyard.

84.
The Dauphine Gateway,
façade on the Oval Courtyard side.

85.
Gateway to the
ballroom staircase.

Oval Courtyard

Retracing our steps to the ballroom wing and passing between the two former guardhouses, we find on our left the entrance to the Oval Courtyard. The wall linking the Tiber Pavilion to its identical pendant (called the Luxembourg Pavilion since the end of the 18th century) has an opening in the centre by the monumental Dauphine Gate or Baptistry Gate (fig. 83 and 84). This gateway consists of two separate parts: a ground floor in rusticated sandstone, re-employing a former drawbridge edifice, created by Primaticcio in 1565 near the moat in the White Horse Courtyard, and an ashlar storey in the form of an arcade surmounted by a four-sided dome in the Mannerist style adorned with sculptures. The façade on the side of the former moat is decorated with large antique masks in white marble.

The Keep or Oval Courtyard, despite the removal of the window mullions and drastic restorations carried out in the 19th century, remains very much as it was after the alterations made by Henri IV in 1600. Turning from left to right, we see first of all, after the Tiber Pavilion, the ballroom wing, with the first four bays corresponding to the building operations undertaken at the start of the 17th century masking the fronts of the upper and lower Saint Saturnin Chapels. Only the two large turrets of this former façade appear in the roof. The ballroom itself (five bays) ends with a square staircase tower, built at the same time (around 1545), pierced on the ground floor by a double door decorated with a pediment, two sculptures, *Minerva* and *Juno*, and a niche containing a bust of the King (put back in the 19th century) (fig. 85).

Here begin the buildings reconstructed by François I in 1528 on either side of the medieval keep (fig. 86). Although the keep matches the neighbouring façades (bands dividing the storeys, opening up of bays, raised roof), it also resembles other keeps in the area by its shape and plan, as well as the arrangement on three floors standing back a

86.
The Oval Courtyard, partial view of the buildings from the Keep to the Serlio Portico.

little from the others, and its rubble masonry, so that it could perhaps date back to the beginning of the 12th century. The surrounding façades, which may have kept some traces on the ground floor of constructions prior to François I, present in the sandstone and mortar rubble structure a decoration of pilasters at irregular intervals and clumsily placed dormer windows with triangular pediments. They nevertheless reveal in 1528 (just like the Golden Gate) a desire to innovate.

Next comes the Serlio Portico (fig. 87) (moved at the time of Henri IV and entirely rebuilt in 1893), which has been given a much more careful treatment in a style very similar to that of the apse of the Saint Saturnin Chapels. It is a kind of triumphal arch,

with two storeys each consisting of three arcades, two of semicircular arches and the other one with a basket arch. Originally it was a staircase and its probable early aspect (between 1531 and 1540) was imagined in 1940 by the architect Albert Bray, following his excavations in the courtyard. Serlio could not possibly have taken part in its construction, both for chronological reasons and because of its style.

Beyond the portico, as far as the Luxembourg Pavilion, Henri IV constructions match the façades of François I. Likewise, the ambulatory gallery on columns which runs from the back of the Golden Gate in front of the François I façades, was extended in front of the Henri IV façades.

87.
The so-called Serlio Portico.

88.
Gilles Guérin.
One of the heads of Mercury on the outer portal of the Oval Courtyard.

89.
South wing of the Offices Courtyard, middle section of the façade on the courtyard side.

90.
One of the bronze mascarons on the Three Faces Fountain at the foot of the façade on the courtyard side of the central pavilion of the south wing of the Offices Courtyard.

91.
Entrance pavilion to the north wing of the Offices Courtyard, façade overlooking the place d'armes.

Offices Courtyard, called Henri IV Courtyard

Facing the entrance to the Oval Courtyard is the courtyard surrounded by the servants' hall and kitchens (1606-1609). It is reached through a wrought-iron gate framed by two sandstone posts surmounted by colossal heads of Mercury (carved by Gilles Guérin, 1639) (fig. 88). On all three sides there are buildings of brick and mortar rubble walls, alternately high and low to break the monotony. The most remarkable parts of these edifices are, on the one hand, the middle pavilion in the south wing, with the front overlooking the courtyard deeply incurved forming a sort of exhedra or theatre (fig. 89), similar to the central block at Grosbois, to the new château at Saint-Germain-en-Laye, or to some of Androuet du Cerceau's plans (on a lower level there are three fountains adorned with three beautiful bronze masks - fig. 90). On the other hand there is the great entrance gate (fig. 91), which on the town side is made entirely of sandstone in rusticated bossage, with its monumental niche. Designed in the manner of a city gate in a very sober style close to that of Salomon de Brosse, it is a forerunner shapewise of the exhedra at the end of the courtyard and, regarding the material employed, it looks like the gate of the Keep Courtyard.

91

89

92

93

92.
The Wing of the Stags Gallery
and the Diana Gallery,
façade overlooking
the Diana Garden.

93.
Detail of the façade of the Wing
of the Stags and Diana Galleries, on the first floor.

Façades overlooking the moat and the Diana Garden

If, after the Baptistry Gate, we continue to walk along the side of the moat, we come on the left, opposite the Offices Courtyard, to some very ordinary buildings in brick and mortar rubble. They were added in several stages in Louis XV's day to the Henri IV buildings of the keeper's lodge, enclosing its courtyard. On this occasion, the Henri IV parts were transformed, with a care for harmony, except at the end of the building, particularly the corner pavilion where they have kept their original aspect. Turning round the right-hand corner we follow the north front of the keeper's lodge, the bays of which were altered in the 18th century and at the time of Napoléon I (large window of the Diana Gallery). The inner façades of these buildings (not normally visible) date from Louis XIV, Louis XV and Louis-Philippe.

The buildings surrounding the Diana Garden are also markedly ill-matched. To the East, the wing of the Diana and Stag Galleries (fig. 92) in brick and stone, in an ornate Mannerist style (*c.* 1600) is the only remaining vestige of Henri IV's constructions encircling on three sides the Box-Tree or Queen's Garden. It consists, on each side of a slightly projecting central block adorned with niches, of twenty windows separated by pilasters on the ground floor and above, tall windows partly cutting into the eaves with alternate triangular and winged pediments, oval niches with shells and fleurons, and small pilasters (fig. 93). It ends on the north side with a corner pavilion, called the Louis-Philippe Pavilion, a pastiche of the Henri-IV style, built in 1833 when the ruins of the former orangery were pulled down. Southwards is the wing containing the State apartments in sandstone ashlar, a very sober construction which acquired its present outline at the time of Louis XV who had it partly brought forward, adding on in 1773 the semicircular rotunda of the Council Chamber (fig. 94). Two of the bays have peculiar smaller windows adorned with wrought-iron balconies, corresponding with the Queen's

94.
Wing of the royal apartments, façade overlooking the garden, corresponding on the first floor to the Throne and Council Rooms.

cabinets on the first and mezzanine floor (the upper windows, oculi in Louis XV's time, were transformed for Marie-Antoinette.) Beyond the Council Chamber rotunda, the wing added alongside the François I Gallery, doubling it in width (1785-1786) copies without any changes the neighbouring sandstone constructions, but the attic was altered under Louis-Philippe (the number of attic windows was doubled).

The side façade of the chapel appearing at a right angle was completely renovated under Charles X, its gallery on the first floor with large arched windows replacing a terrace. Next comes a staircase tower (François I period) with, on the ground floor, the famous Egyptian caryatid door, its pediment adorned with groups of putti holding up the coat-of-arms and monogram of the King (fig. 95), then the Arms Pavilion (built under François I but heavily restored) and finally, set back, one of the side walls of the Jeu de Paume.

The garden itself, which had been designed in the informal style by Napoléon I and then by Louis-Philippe, is embellished chiefly by the fountain giving it its name. Created in 1603 by Francini, stripped of some of its bronzes during the Revolution, partly restored by Napoléon in 1813 (without the dogs), it retrieved its original aspect in the 20th century. The statue of Diana, from the Antique, is not the one placed there in 1603 (see below p. 155), but another copy made for Marly in 1684 by the Kellers and brought here in 1813. The dogs and the stagheads are due to the sculptor Pierre Biard (1603) (fig. 96). In the garden there are two other sculptures: a *Venus Italica* after Canova (which entered the château in 1824) and *The Saltarelle Dancer* by Sanson, in bronze, cast by V. Thiébaut (entered Fontainebleau in 1876).

95.
The Egyptian
caryatid doorway.

96.
The Diana
Fountain.

95

Plan of
the ground floor

1. Way in
2. Napoléon III's theatre

Musée Napoléon Ier
3. Room IX : Madame Mère
4. Room X : Joseph
5. Room XI : Louis
6. Room XII : Jérôme
7. Room XIII : Élisa
8. Room XIV : Pauline
9. Room XV : Caroline
10. Way out
11. Trinity Chapel

Private apartments
12. The Emperor's antechamber
13. The Emperor's first drawing-room
14. The Emperor's second drawing-room
15. Méneval's bedroom
16. The Emperor's wardrobe room
17. The Keeper of the Emperor's Privy Seal room
18. The Emperor's bedchamber
19. Passage room
20. The Emperor's office; third room
21. The Emperor's office; second room
22. The Emperor's office; first room
23. Col de cygne antechamber
24. Topographical room

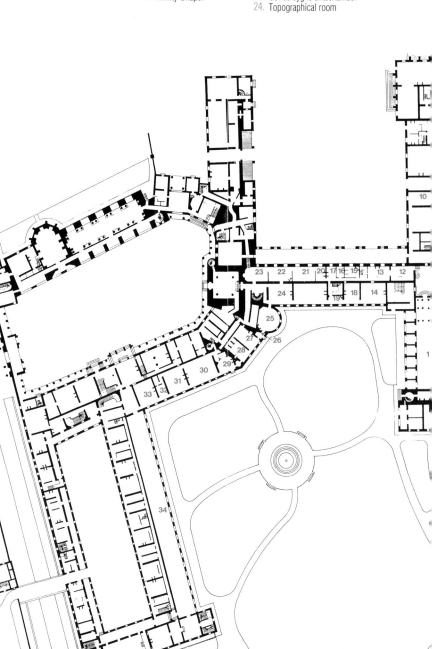

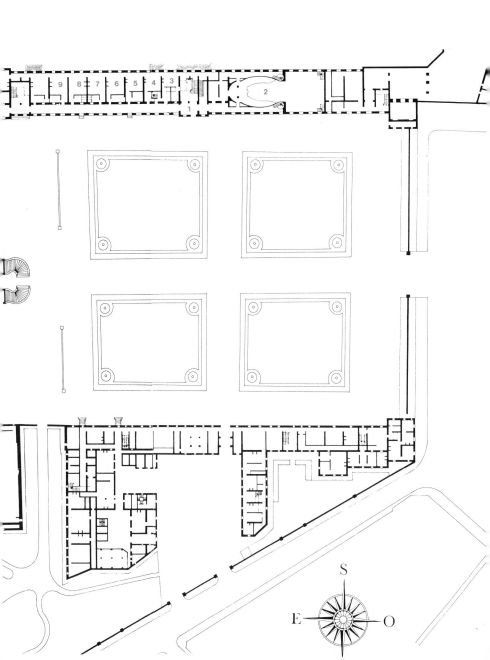

Plan of
the first floor

Musée Napoléon Ier
35. Corridor
36. Room I: Napoléon, Emperor and King
37. Room II: The ceremonial of the Imperial table
38. Room III: Gifts to the Emperor
39. Room IV: The Emperor in battle
40. Room V: Day-to-day life of the Emperor
41. Room VI: Marie-Louise
42. Room VII: The Roi de Rome
43. Room VIII: The Roi de Rome
44. Room VIIIb: The Roi de Rome
45. Central staircase

State Apartments
46. Stuccoed staircase
47. Antechamber of the Great Events Gallery
48. Great Events Gallery
49. Plates Gallery
50. Horseshoe vestibule
51. Trinity Chapel (tribune)

Renaissance Rooms
52. François I Gallery
53. Passage between the François I Gallery and the guardroom
54. Rotunda
55. Bedroom of Madame d'Etampes or the King's staircase
56. Ballroom

**Apartment of
Madame de Maintenon**
57. Bedchamber
58. Cabinet
59. Loggia and large drawing-room
60. Antechamber
61. Vestibule
62. Antechamber of the former theatre, known as Louis XV's small drawing-room

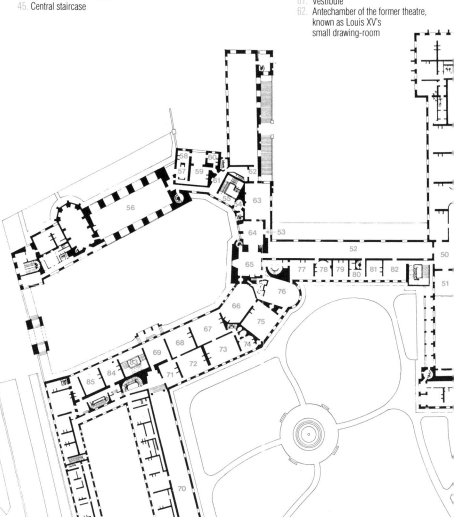

The sovereigns'
state apartments
63. Guardroom
64. First Saint Louis Chamber
65. Second Saint Louis Chamber
66. Louis XIII Chamber
67. François I Chamber
68. Tapestries room
69. The Empress's antechamber
70. The Diana Gallery
71. White drawing-room
   or the Queen's drawing-room
72. The Queen's gamesroom
   or the Empress's large drawing-room

73. The Empress's bedchamber
74. The Queen's boudoir
75. Throne room
76. Council Chamber
77. The Emperor's bedchamber
78. The Emperor's small bedroom
79. The Emperor's private drawing-room,
   known as the Abdication Room
80. Passage to the baths and bathroom
   of the Emperor
81. Drawing-room for the Emperor's aides de camp
82. The Emperor's antechamber

The Queen's staircase
Hunts apartment
83. The Queen's staircase
84. The Prince Imperial's drawing-room
85. The Prince Imperial's bedroom

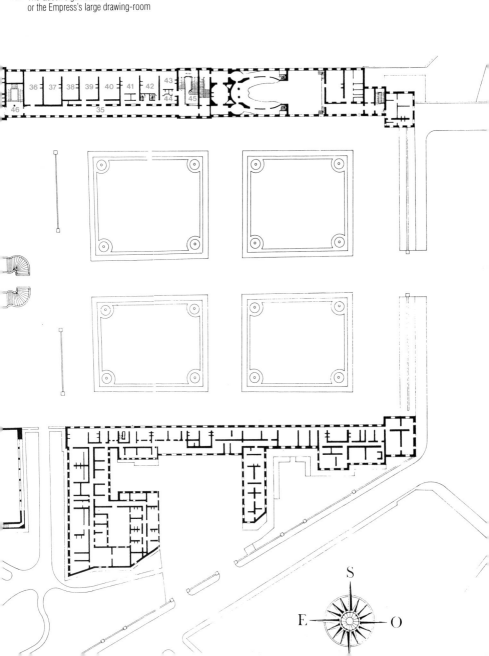

97.
Laurent-Charles
Maréchal,
The Artist,
stained-glass
window.

State Apartments

Since 1986, the visitor enters through the central pavilion of the Louis XV wing, walks along the ground-floor corridor and climbs the stucco staircase (1866-1868). Called the Philippe-Auguste Staircase owing to the plaster statue of this king after Jaley which adorned it in the 19th century, it is lit by a very fine Louis-XV lantern (entered in 1868), attributed to J. Caffieri. The ramp is a copy of the one on the chapel staircase dating from the 17th century.

Antechamber of the Great Events Gallery

The stained-glass window (fig. 97), designed by Laurent-Charles Maréchal, representing *The Artist*, was bought by Napoléon III at the Exposition Universelle in 1867. It was enlarged and installed in the middle bay in 1869, taken down in 1939 and put back in place in 1984.

Paintings: various pictures recreate the appearance this room had at the end of the Second Empire: J. Lemaire, *Women dancing in a Palace* (from the collection of the Duc de Penthièvre at the Hôtel de Toulouse); also by Lemaire, *Peristyle of a Palace in Ruins*; J.B. Oudry, *Lise, Louis XV's Dog* and *Mignonne and Sylvie, Dogs belonging to Louis XV,* 1728; P. Domenchin de Chavanne, two *Landscapes* (painted in 1737 for the Queen's cabinet at Fontainebleau); N.H. Jeaurat de Bertry, *A Drum and a Sword*.

Furniture: lantern (Chaumont, 1804); two vases called the Achilles vases, in Sèvres porcelain (1865).

The Great Events Gallery

This was created at the time of Napoléon III in place of a staircase and a vestibule, in order to join the Plates Gallery to the Louis XV wing. The Emperor conceived the idea of decorating the walls with pictures representing historical events which had taken place at Fontainebleau, hence its name of the Great Events Gallery, but only the ceiling adorned with the Imperial coat-of-arms was finished (painted by Alexandre Denuelle in 1866-1867).

In 1976, this room was rearranged as a picture gallery, as it used to be at the end of the Second Empire.

Paintings: school of N. dell'Abbate, *Threshing Corn* (fig. 98); G.B. Viola, *Landscape* (coll. of Louis XIV); F. Albani, *Apollo tending the Flocks of King Admetus* (coll. of Louis XIV); by the same artist, *The Triumph of Cybele* (idem); M. Rosselli, *Rest on the Flight into Egypt*; G.B. Castiglione, *Jacob departing from Mesopotamia*; D. Teniers,

98.
Nicolo dell'Abbate (school of), *Threshing Corn.*

Village Fête with People playing Bowls (coll. of Louis XIV); C. Decker, *Landscape*; G.P. Panini, *Ruins*; J.B. Oudry, *Misse and Turlu, two of Louis XV's Dogs*, (1725); by the same artist, *Gredinet, Petite-fille, Charlotte, Dogs belonging to Louis XV* (1727); P. Subleyras, *The Martyrdom of Saint Hippolytus*; A.J. Vernet, *Seascape, Setting Sun* (1753); J.M. Vien, *The Cupid-Seller* (1763); L.J.F. Lagrenée, *Justice and Clemency*; by the same artist, *Kindness and Generosity* (1765) (overdoors for the Château de Choisy); also *The Dauphin dying surrounded by his Family, the Duc de Bourgogne presenting him with the Crown of Immortality* (Salon of 1767) – the Dauphin, Louis XV's only son, died at Fontainebleau on 20 December 1765. G. van Spaendonck, *Flowers on an alabaster Pedestal with a bronze* Vase (1785); R. Lefèvre, *Venus disarming Cupid* (Salon of an IV – 1795): C. Van Loo, *Ruins of a Gothic Church with a snow-covered Bridge in the Distance* (an IX - 1801); C. Landon, *Leda, Pollux and Helen* (Salon of 1806); A.C. Haudebourg-Lescot, *Kissing the Feet of Saint Peter at Saint Peter's Basilica in Rome* (Salon of 1812); A.H. Dunouy, *Vesuvius in Eruption in 1813* (Salon of 1817); also, *View of the Bay of Naples from the Coast of the Posilippo*

(1819); A.L.R. Millin du Perreux, *Henri IV raising Sully to his Feet at Fontainebleau* (1819) (fig. 99), taken from the Diana Gallery (see below p. 118); J.F. van Dael, *Flowers and Fruit* (1823); A.M.L. Grandpierre-Deverzy, *Monaldeschi imploring Christina of Sweden for Pardon at Fontainebleau* (1824) (for details of this episode, see below p. 153); D. Roberts, *Ambulatory round the Choir of Chartres Cathedral*, two watercolours; M. Jacobber, *Flowers and Fruit* (1849).

Furniture: some of the furniture from the apartment of the Queen Mothers (or of the Pope), now undergoing restoration, are on display here: Louis-XIV chairs in gilded wood, partly 17th-century (four armchairs), partly 19th-century (sofa, two armchairs by Jacob-Desmalter, 1836); two armchairs, one attributed to F. Foliot, *circa* 1770, the other one a copy by Sené and Laurent for Madame Élisabeth's bedroom at Fontainebleau in 1791 (bought back from Gérard, 1804); chest-of-drawers with marquetry by Riesener, *circa* 1775-1780 (purchased from Legendre, 1804); commode "with fasces" by Stöckel and Beneman for the Council Chamber at Compiègne, 1786.

99.
Alexandre-Louis-Robert Millin du Perreux, *Henri IV raising Sully to his Feet at Fontainebleau.*

Plates Gallery (fig. 100)

Created in 1840, it was first called the Fresco Gallery and acquired its present name during the Second Empire.

Decoration: the Gallery was lined with panelling in the Renaissance style in 1840. On the ceiling and walls, there are twenty-one fragments of oil paintings on plaster from the vaulted roof of the Diana Gallery, by Ambroise Dubois and his assistants, *circa* 1600-1605 (see below p. 118). These paintings were taken down in 1810, transferred on to canvas, restored by Alaux and installed here in 1840.

Furniture: one hundred and twenty-eight plates in Sèvres porcelain belonging to the "Historic Service" of Fontainebleau (1839-1844), representing various events which took place at Fontainebleau, views of the forest and the castle, at different periods, as well as foreign countries visited by Louis-Philippe: North America, England, Sicily. Gilt bronze brackets for a carcel lamp, Chaumont et Marquis, 1840-1841. Sèvres porcelain cabinet commemorating the marriage of the Duc d'Orléans (fig. 101), with scenes painted by Develly (entered Fontainebleau in 1841). A vaulted vestibule and a narrow corridor lead to the Horseshoe Vestibule.

100. The Plates Gallery.

101.
Cabinet commemorating the marriage of the Duc d'Orléans and Princess Helen von Mecklemburg-Schwerin, manufacture de Sèvres, Louis-Philippe period.

Horseshoe Vestibule

Decoration: three of the doors date back to the reign of Louis XIII: the door leading to the terrace, the door of the chapel tribune and the door of the François I Gallery (fig. 102). Their wooden panels were carved by Jean Gobert in 1639, but the name of the sculptor responsible for the elaborate stone surrounds is unknown. The rest was decorated in Louis-Philippe's time: the ceiling; the frieze adorned with the monograms of various sovereigns by the sculptor Jean-Baptiste-Louis Plantar (1834); three doors copied from the one at the entrance to the François I Gallery by the joiner Lambert Lefébure en 1833.

Furniture: this dates from the Second Empire. Armchair, table and benches in carved oak, inspired by the Louis-XIII doors, Grohé, 1862-1863, from drawings by the architect Victor Ruprich-Robert; lantern in the Louis-XVI style (entered in 1860), 18th-century Boulle cartel (provenance: Veuve David sale, 1862).

102

102.
The Horseshoe
vestibule, door to
the François I Gallery.

Trinity Chapel

(fig 103)

History: the present-day edifice replaced the chapel of the monastery of the Trinitarians (or Mathurins) founded by Saint Louis. Construction began at the end of François I's reign and was completed at the time of Henri II. Nothing remains of the interior decoration of this period, except for the arcades at the back of the choir (invisible from the chapel) and the two great shields at each end of the vault, one surrounded by the collar of the Golden Fleece, the other by that of the Order of Saint Michael.

In 1605 King Henri IV had the present vault built (fig. 104) and Martin Fréminet was put in charge of the new decoration. He based his plan on the writings of a Jesuit, Père Richeôme. According to Don Morin, Fréminet started to carry out his project on 1 May 1608. On 20 August 1608 work was in full swing and the Annunciation scene, situated above the choir, was already well advanced if not finished.

103

104

103.
Trinity Chapel.

104.
Vaulted ceiling
of the Chapel painted by
Martin Fréminet.

107

105

105.
The high altar

106.
The royal tribune.

107.
Jean Dubois,
The Holy Trinity at the Moment of the Deposition of the Cross, painting on the high altar.

106

After the death of Henri IV, in 1613, the sculptor Barthélemy Tremblay undertook to decorate in plaster, from designs by Fréminet, the frames of fourteen pictures in the chapel periphery, which suggests that the vault was by then complete. Fréminet himself provided ideas for paintings, as proved by a recent discovery of six small paintings in his hand in collections at the Louvre. It is not known however to what extent he took part in the mural decoration or whether his death in 1619 was responsible for work coming to a halt. In any case nothing more was done until 1628 when work resumed and lasted for another ten years or so. The sculptor Francesco Bordoni was then made responsible for the high altar (fig. 105) at a cost of thirty-five thousand *livres*, using the plans left by Fréminet. Wooden panelling and railings shutting off the chapels were done by Jean Maujan, ordinary joiner of buildings (who passed on some of the work to the sculptor Robert Andry at the beginning of 1629); the sculptor Germain Gissey, in September 1629, undertook to finish the mural decoration begun by his father-in-law Tremblay (who had apparently completed three quarters of the work already because he had received one thousand eight hundred *livres* out of the two thousand four hundred promised). Gissey joined the painters Jean Bertrand and Robert Cammel "concerning the paintings and sculptures for the great chapel", but their association broke up in December 1631. The year of dedication, 1633, is inscribed on the pediment of the high altar. The account books kept for the period 1639-1642 mention however that the entrance-door on the ground floor was not installed until 1639 by the joiner Antoine Girault (when Gobert was doing the woodwork for the doors of the vestibule on the first floor and for the royal tribune) (fig. 106), and also the wainscotting and that the picture above the altar, painted at a cost of five hundred *livres* by Jean Dubois, son of Ambroise, and representing the Holy Trinity at the Descent from the Cross, was not executed until 1642 (fig. 107). The fact that the sculptor Bordoni was paid in 1642 for the coloured marble paving for the two oratories in the "great chapel" proves clearly that he had previously been responsible for the great paving of the nave, as was the tradition since the beginning of the 17th century.

In 1664, at the start of Louis XIV's reign, when the Mathurins regained possession of their church of which they had been deprived in 1608 when work had started, Colbert had a small choir arranged for them on the left of the altar, by demolishing two chapels situated beneath a terrace. The walls of this choir were panelled by André Gobert. In 1667 a black marble plaque was placed near the main altar (still *in situ*) recording that Louis XIV had made an endowment for six masses to be celebrated each year for the soul of Queen Anne d'Autriche who died in 1666. Then, from 1679 to 1681, the sculptor Girardon made a new tabernacle in marble and gilt bronze with bas-reliefs representing the Holy Trinity, the two founders of the Trinitarian order, Saint Félix de Valois and Saint Jean de Matha and the four Evangelists (this altar is now in the Saint Louis Church at Fontainebleau). In 1688, the construction of the staircase to the François I Gallery led to the demolition of the first chapel on the right on entering (medieval vestiges were then discovered). In 1702-1703, Guy-Louis Vernansal received five hundred and seventy-eight *livres* to repair part of the paintings in the vault near the altar, slightly damaged by a fire in the Arms Pavilion.

In the 18th century few transformations were made. In 1740 an enlargement was planned which would have provided room for a transept, enabling the Mathurins choir to be moved behind the altar. All that was done however was to add an extra bay in 1741 to the 17th-century royal tribune supported by ten columns, which was considered too cramped, and to install benches and two niches or "lanterns" for the king and queen, more spacious than before (they already existed in Louis XIV's day but had no doubt been altered). Moreover, elaborate wrought-iron balconies, made by the locksmith Parent, were also set up in front of four bays on the first floor of the nave, between the tribune and the balconies intended for the King's Music. The musicians used a rather narrow tribune (above the small Mathurins choir), the roof of which was raised when the old organ (it was said, in 1731, to have come from the old chapel of Versailles) was succeeded, between 1772 and 1774, by a small new 8-foot instrument, due to the organ-maker François-Henry Cliquot, installed in a Louis-XVI style case carved by Boullet the Younger. At the same time, new tiered seats were put up for the musicians. The King also gave orders in 1771 for the tribune lanterns to be removed.

At the time of Louis XVI in 1779, it was thought necessary to replace the murals in poor condition by others. Rather than painting directly on a plastered wall as before, moveable paintings on canvas were preferred. Jean-Baptiste-Marie Pierre decided to reproduce the former subjects, with the exception of two, *Joseph and the Angel* and *The Temptation*, which he changed for a *Nativity* and *The Adoration of the Magi* and divided the commission for fourteen paintings among seven artists: Taraval, Robin, Jollain, Lagrenée the Younger, Renou, Durameau and Amédée Van Loo. As Robin was only able to produce one canvas, Bardin was chosen to paint the second one. Presented at the Salon of 1781 (except those of Durameau which were not exhibited until the Salon of 1789), the pictures were hung here in 1783. Pierre commissioned Regnault to do a new altar painting, but this work did not reach Fontainebleau (kept at the Louvre).

At the time of the Revolution the chapels possessed a copy of the *Marriage of Saint Catherine* by Correggio and a *Virgin Mary* by Stella. The reredos was then partly broken up; what remained of the tabernacle was removed to the parish church of Fontainebleau (it is still there), the two great statues of kings were taken to the Louvre and the gilt bronze ornaments disappeared.

When Napoléon decided to make the palace fit to receive Pope Pius VII, the architects Percier and Fontaine asked for the statues to be brought back and reinstalled there. Napoléon merely had a new tabernacle made; in 1812 Hurtault the architect entrusted Morisot the joiner, Moench the painter and the Delafontaine bronzesmiths with this task.

The chapel needed a complete overhaul which was undertaken between 1824 and 1830 in the reigns of Louis XVIII and Charles X by the architect Jean-Baptiste

Lepère (fig. 108). The side chapels on the right were completely rebuilt with an ambulatory gallery on the first floor instead of the former 16th-century terrace. The organ tribune was raised. Work inside the nave radically transformed the former mural decoration: the twelve oval pictures of Louis XVI's day in their old frames (the two by Durameau were never put back after 1789) were replaced by plain plastered pier panels, and the former carved wooden chapel railings were removed. All the carvings kept were restored by Lambert-Théophile Lefébure. In 1826 the altar painting by Regnault finally supplanted the one by Jean Dubois.

The July Monarchy left everything as it was (the Jean Dubois painting was put back in 1839) and then, during the Second Empire, new renovations started in response to the Emperor's wish to enhance the place where he had been christened. The painter Théodore Lejeune did a considerable amount of restoration on Fréminet's pictures in 1854. The oval paintings, sent back to the Louvre in 1828 and dispersed to various places, were once again assembled by the Direction des Musées, except for the one by Jollain, *The Presentation in the Temple*, which had been badly damaged by fire at the Palais-Royal in 1848. A work on the same theme, painted by Lazerges, was hung where the missing picture had been, but none were ordered for the two pier panels of the tribune, altered during the Restoration. From 1856-1859 Paccard the architect managed to carry out part of his plan. In particular he suggested that the oval pictures should be returned to their original frames, but had to abandon his project in face of the reticence of purists who thought it inappropriate to treat the works of Renou, Lagrenée, Taraval and others "executed in the false conventional style of the previous century" (A.J. du Pays) on the same level as the imposing paintings of Fréminet. The inscription on the reredos, effaced long before, was repainted. The railings round the ground-floor chapels were reinstalled (restored by the Huber brothers) and almost all the gilt bronze ornaments of the altar and the reredos were remade, as well as the attributes of the large angels in patinated bronze (by the bronzesmith Vincent, then by Eck

108.
Artist unknown,
*The Trinity Chapel undergoing
Restoration* c. 1825.
(Fontainebleau, Musée
national du château).

and Durand) from models of the Huber brothers. A statue forming a font in white marble, *Meditation*, by L. Daumas (1864) entered in 1866.

The 20th century in turn left its stamp on the decoration of the chapel. Around 1930 some of the 18th-century canvases, which had long been the subject of scorn, were taken out of storage and hung on the walls unframed. Then, between 1964 and 1968 the Malraux Cultural Affairs Programme Act provided an opportunity for wide-scale operations: the restoration of the paintings on the vaulted ceiling and the Cliquot organ (by the organ-maker Kern), the restitution between the bays on the first floor of the former decorative scheme destroyed during the Restoration. Despite the difficulties encountered, the architect R. de Cidrac reinstalled the upper part of the east wall. After a long interruption, his successor, B. Collette, remodel-

led the plans in 1978. Starting with the west wall, he remade the glass panes prior to 1824, completed and put back the side balconies and had the camaieu figures repainted on the ground-floor panelling. Thus, today, the 18th-century paintings (except for one untraced) are displayed in a decorative setting similar to the one existing at the end of the 18th century.

110

Description of the decoration

• Vault: the theme of this decoration is the story of the Redemption of Man. Starting at the tribune, it depicts in succession: *The Apparition of the Lord to Noah as he leaves the Ark* (the first revelation of Divine Mercy); *Fire* (or Choleric Temperament); *The Fall of the Rebel Angels* (the original sin which led to the Fall of Man); *Air* (or Sanguine Temperament); *Christ on Judgement Day, surrounded by the seven principal Intelligences and Justice* (fig. 109); *Water* (or Phlegmatic Temperament); *The Angel Gabriel sent by God to announce the Incarnation*; *Earth* (or Melancholic Temperament); *The Gathering of the Righteous in Limbo awaiting the Coming of the Son of God*; behind the altar screen, above (only partly visible), *The Annunciation* (the new Alliance between God and Man). On either side, the tall upright figures are the ancestors of the Virgin Mary, the Kings of Judah (Saul, David, Solomon, Rehoboam, Abijah, Asa, Jehosha-

109.

phat, Jehoram); the recumbent grisaille figures are the patriarchs and prophets who proclaimed the coming of Christ. *The Virtues* are the theme of the oval panels: *Faith* and *Hope* in the corners nearest the altar; *Charity* and *Religion* in the corners on the tribune side; between the Prophets there are six other figures of Virtues.

The two large escutcheons, dating from Henri II, were later flanked by angels attributed to Barthélemy Tremblay: above the altar, the coat-of-arms of Henri IV (France and Navarre) surrounded by the collar of the Golden Fleece; above the tribune, the arms of Marie de Médicis (Florence and Austria) surrounded by the collar of Saint Michael (fig. 110). Monograms are scattered over the vault: H (Henri), M (Marie), H and M, HB (Henri de Bourbon) and Greek lambdas (Louis XIII).

• Side walls (restored as they were in 1789): on the side of the White Horse Courtyard, starting at the altar: *The Sibyl of Cumae* and *The Nativity* by Taraval, *The Adoration of the Magi* by Bardin, *The Presentation in the Temple* by Lazerges, *Jesus among the Doctors* by Jollain, *The Baptism of Christ* and *The Marriage at Cana* by Jean-Jacques Lagrenée. Returning from the tribune to the altar, on the right, *The Tribute Money* and *Supper at Simon's House* by Amédée Van Loo, *Jesus and the Samaritan* and *Jesus with the Woman taken in Adultery* by Renou; (*Jesus cleansing the Temple* is missing;) *The Healing of the Paralytic* by Durameau (fig. 111); *The Transfiguration* by Robin.

• High altar: altar piece, *The Holy Trinity* by Jean Dubois; statues by Francesco Bordoni: on the left, *Charlemagne* with the features of Henri IV; on the right, *Saint Louis* with the features of Louis XIII; at the top, four angels, two of them bearing incense, the other two symbolising Justice and Perseverance (fig. 112).

Furniture: communion table from the Chartrettes Church (entered in 1964).

111

112

109.
Martin Fréminet,
Christ on Judgement Day surrounded by the seven principal Intelligences and Justice, central compartment of the vaulted ceiling of the Chapel.

110.
Shield bearing the arms of Henri IV and Marie de Médicis at the south end of the vaulted ceiling, above the tribune.

111.
Durameau, *Jesus healing the Paralytic.*

112.
Francesco Bordoni, two of the angels at the top of the high altar, bronze.

113.
François I Gallery.

114.
Antoine Pierretz,
detail from
the carved panelling
in the François I Gallery,
engraving, 1646.

Renaissance Rooms

François I Gallery (fig. 113).

In the 16th century, this was the Great Gallery, until the start of the 17th century when it became the François I or Small Gallery. In the 18th century it was generally called the *"Galerie des Réformés"*, though it is not known to which particular event this name refers, perhaps to officers discharged by Louis XIV in 1664).

History: this Gallery is situated in a wing erected in 1528 to link the royal apartments and the Trinitarian Monastery, founded by Saint Louis near the royal residence.

The decoration was entrusted some years after its construction to Rosso who was assisted by a team of French, Italian and Flemish painters and sculptors. According to the *Comptes* (accounts), the stuccowork started in March 1535 and was finished in May 1537. The frescoes were begun in 1536. As for the joinery, Rosso called upon an Italian, Francisco Seibec de Carpi who in 1539 carved the wainscotting (fig. 114) in walnut and a parquet floor (he could also have been responsible some years earlier for the ceiling).

The gallery was not decorated in a strictly symmetrical manner, for an architectural transformation soon altered the plans. Indeed, in 1528 the centre of the Gallery was marked by two small projecting cabinets. In 1534-1535 though, the king had a terraced building erected along the south wall on the pond side, intended for kitchens and pantries on the ground floor. As the new terrace could serve as an outside passage, the small south cabinet was separated from the Gallery before 1539, the year when the panelling was installed. The problem is complicated by the fact that the fresco which has taken its place is not by Rosso but by Primaticcio who had painted another fresco in the small north cabinet. For lack of proof, one can only say that Primaticcio's participation in this decoration

could have occurred before or after the death of Rosso. In any case, when work was completed, this decoration had the following aspect: from east to west a succession of windows determined the location of seven bays, two groups of six frescoes by Rosso, relating "histories", interrupted by a central bay devoted to mythological scenes painted by Primaticcio; at the east and west ends,

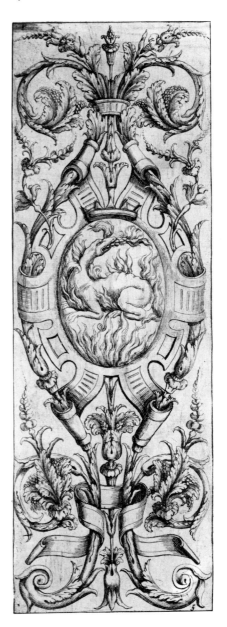

there were also mythological scenes: two paintings on canvas by Rosso: *Venus and Cupid* (east); *Venus and Bacchus* (west). The latter picture is known through a version held by the State Museum of the Grand Duchy of Luxemburg.

Apart from the mythological scenes (only *Danaë* remains in place), the "historical" cycle is still intact in all its astonishing complexity. It was no doubt imagined by a learned scholar at the court of François I, nurtured in the writings of Antiquity and emblem books. Some have suggested that it was Rosso himself, or the ambassador Lazare de Baïf, Guillaume Budé or André Alciat, but the mystery has never been solved. The literary sources (Ovid, Hyginus, Nicander of Colophon ...), from whom certain stories are taken, have sometimes been identified, but the allegories hidden in the legends are not clear and the general meaning of the overall decoration escapes us. According to studies made in the 20th century by several experts (notably Tervarent, Panofsky, Chastel), the frescoes can be grouped into two distinct parts: in short, on the side of the royal apartments, the subjects seem more concerned with humanity in general, the inevitability of war, the burden of Fate, old age, disaster and death as the lot of mankind; on the chapel side, the themes are those of the grandeur of the institution of monarchy in the person of the king. Monarchy means devotion, the guarantee of the unity of the nation as realised in Antiquity, and it is dedicated to the service of the people.

Rosso treats these subjects in a highly original style: clashing colours typical of Florentine Mannerism, complex compositions, often tense and dramatic, and a taste for the bizarre. The influence of Michaelangelo transpires not only in the stuccowork, but again in the frescoes (the figures have a sculptural look). Moreover, a certain humour is evident in numerous details. The variety of motifs on the framework is just as characteristic (Primaticcio was never to display such flights of imagination). One type of ornament is the strapwork, which was to play a role of capital importance in the history of decorative art and Rosso seems to have been the first to have employed it systematically.

Since the 16th century diverse changes have altered the initial appearance of the gallery. In 1639 a door was pierced in the west wall leading to the new horseshoe vestibule (a painting on canvas by Rosso was removed). The construction in 1688 of the chapel staircase and the opening of a door led to a remodelling of the stuccowork situated on the left of the Sacrifice fresco (by the sculptor François Besson). In 1701 Louis XIV replaced the two most daring subjects by pictures painted by Louis de Boulogne. Rosso's painting at the eastern end was supplanted by *Zephyr and Flora*, in the small north room Primaticcio's mural of *Jupiter and Semele* gave way to *Minerva and the Arts near the Bust of François I*. Guibert says that around 1710, Poerson painted a fresco above the vestibule door of *Victory crowning François I and History writing down his Actions on the Wings of Time* (see fig. 118). After the frescoes had been restored in 1730-1731 by Jean-Baptiste Van Loo, assisted notably by Chardin, a new alteration was decided in 1757: to make communication inside the royal apartment easier it was decided to pierce some large doors. In order to do so, the whole of the eastern end of the gallery was remodelled by the architect Gabriel (fig. 115, 116).

Then in 1785, the small north cabinet was condemned when the gallery was doubled in size by a wing to provide rooms for the king's private apartments. The windows looking on to the Diana Garden were blocked up (unfortunately still shutting out the light on the decoration on the south wall). Where a large bay had once been, it was thought sufficient in 1786 to repeat the motifs on the frame of the Danaë fresco, placing there Boulogne's picture representing Minerva, taken from the former small cabinet. Above, a chimney was created with Egyptian chimeras in lead, cast by Thomire from models of the sculptor Roland. Berthélemy, then at work on the queen's apartment, was ordered to restore the frescoes once again, under the supervision of Pierre the painter. Cupboards stood against the panelling so that the shops, set up when the Court was visiting, were all alike. The Revolution left the Château untouched. Apparently only the

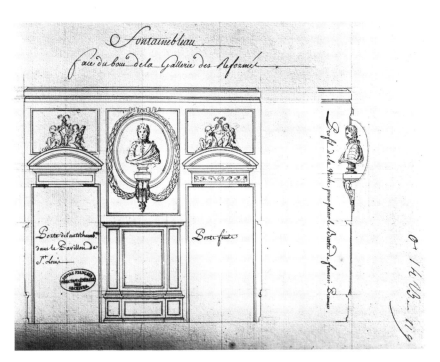

115.
Design for the east end
of the François I Gallery
by the architect
Ange-Jacques Gabriel,
1757, drawing
(Paris, Archives nationales).

116.
East end
of the François I Gallery.

fleur-de-lis cartouches on the panels were replaced. Napoléon got rid of the merchants' cupboards and transformed the gallery into a room of Illustrious Men (*Salle des Illustres*). There he put busts of generals and great men, as well as sixty drawings by Bagetti illustrating his campaigns. A bust of Henri IV was set in the niche at the end, which since 1757 had contained one of François I. During the Restoration the gallery remained unchanged, though the busts too reminiscent of the imperial regime were removed (fig. 117). It was not until the end of Louis-Philippe's reign, from 1846 onwards, that overall restoration of the gallery was undertaken. The ceiling was raised and the space gained was used for a papier-mâché frieze in the Renaissance taste (commissioned from the sculptor Klagmann) (fig. 118). Auguste Couder began restoring the paintings, the wall panelling was renovated and completed, the 1786 chimney was removed and a new

parquet floor was laid. The Second Republic having decided to destroy the frieze, Napoléon III, who brought to an end the work on the gallery between 1853 and 1860, had it replaced by a painted frieze. The joiner Beaudet made some new french windows. As the work begun by Couder had been severely criticised, the task of restoring the frescoes was entrusted to Alaux. He repainted them entirely, using the encaustic technique and added two new subjects: *The Nymph of Fontainebleau* (facing Danae) and *The Dispute between Minerva and Neptune* (above the entrance). Finally, from 1960 to 1965, Rosso's frescoes, which had been painted over by Alaux, were brought to light during restoration work. André Malraux was responsible for this "resurrection" which was achieved with spectacular results by O. Binenbaum (for the frescoes) and J.P. Ledeur (for the stuccowork). At the same time the Napoléon III frieze was taken away

117.
The François I Gallery in 1840, engraving by Alfred Guesdon.

and the ceiling was lowered, unfortunately though not to its original height.

Description of the mural decoration:
the descriptions follow the order of the visit, whereas, in the mind of the creator, the decoration should be viewed from east to west, starting at the sovereign's bedchamber.

• *West end*.
16th-century stuccowork. The subjects of the medallions have not been elucidated: on the right, we see *Fortune giving a Drink to a Prince* (Caesar ?), on the left, a scene which could be the night before the Taking of Troy. Overdoor: *Dispute between Minerva and Neptune* by Alaux (*c.* 1860), from an engraving of the 16th century.

• *First north bay: A Sacrifice*.
Main picture. A high priest wearing a mitre is standing close to a blazing altar stamped with the royal 'F'. Among the crowd are vase-bearers, seated women with babies in their arms, old men, one of whom on the left is carried on an armchair by a young man seen from behind. Next to him a child is holding a crutch. Frame. Frescoes: below, a round of dryads. Stuccoes: on the right, the sacrifice of a ram, on the left, fragment of the sacrifice of a bull (altered in the reign of Louis XIV).

The presence of a large number of children, of wine-vessel bearers as though to celebrate the rites of birth, as well as dryads associated with fecundity, has suggested an evocation of the birth of François I, predicted to his mother by Saint Francis of Paola (1416-1507), who possibly appears here as a high priest. The reputation of the miracles wrought by this saint would explain the presence of aged men imploring to be healed. It has also been suggested that, like Aaron, the mediator between God and the chosen

118.
The west end of the François I Gallery, as it was in 1849 following work undertaken by Louis-Philippe, drawn by the architect Abel Blouet (Paris, Bibiothèque nationale); the carved frieze at the top corresponds to the heightening of the ceiling.

people, this high priest is none other than the king of France himself who, consecrated and anointed, is both priest and thaumaturge.

• *First south bay*:
Ignorance chased away (fig. 119).
Main picture. Men and women blindfolded are standing on clouds and feeling their way along. Others, seated, appear to be prostrate. On the right, entering a temple, François I as a laurel-wreathed *imperator* is holding the sword in his right hand and a book under his left arm. An engraving tells us that the pediment of the door bore the inscription *Ostium Jovis*, i.e. Jupiter's door. Between the columns, two large ewers on which the words *Mali* and *Boni* used to appear. Frame. Stuccoes: on the right and left, a male and a female satyr accompanied by child satyrs; below, Venus in a conch-shell (the figure of Venus has disappeared). Frescoes: above, four women, one of them playing the flute; below, animals (turkeys and rodents).

Since the 17th century, an allusion is usually seen in this panel to the King's cultural policy, to the creation of the Collège de France and the Imprimerie Royale. Another interpretation is that the King, urged by his faith, has come to ask God for Enlightment on the Knowledge of Good and Evil, for his blind people, since their ignorance lets loose the vices (the stucco satyrs could symbolise lust).

• *Second north bay*:
The Royal Elephant.
Main picture (fig. 120). An elephant trapped with a caparison adorned with fleurs-de-lis and the royal F, and a frontal strap with the salamander escutcheon, appears on an arena. There is a stork at his feet. Around him are three young men: one with thunder, another with a trident and dolphin (very faint) and another with a three-headed dog. On the left are numerous spectators. Above right: a statue? Frame. Frescoes: right and left, the rapt of mortals by gods changed into animals: *Jupiter changed into a Bull abducting Europa* (left); *Saturn, disguised as a Horse seizing Phylira* (right). Stucco: below, *Alexander cutting the Gordian Knot.*

The elephant is an allegorical portrait of François I. Since Antiquity this animal has symbolised wisdom and royalty (an antique coin of Caesar shows an elephant trampling on a serpent). The stork would be the symbol of filial piety. Around the elephant, Saturn's three sons represent the elements: Jupiter (Fire), Neptune (Water), Pluto (Earth). The bearded man below on the left, dressed in green, is thought to be Rosso himself. The scenes of rapt could symbolise bestial passions confronted by royal wisdom. The panel would thus mean that King François I was wise, virtuous and master of the elements, so that his power was universal. The imperial vocation of French monarchy is suggested implicitly, as the bas-relief of the Gordian Knot appears to testify. François I could be a new Alexander, whereas, in the opposite mural, he appears as a new Caesar.

119. Rosso. *Ignorance chased away*, fresco and stucco.

120. Rosso, *The Royal Elephant*, fresco.

121. Rosso, *The Fire*, fresco and stucco.

• *Second south bay*:
Unity of the State.
Main picture. François I, clad as a Roman emperor crowned with laurels, is holding a pomegranate. Kneeling at his feet, a child presents him with other pomegranates. The sovereign is surrounded by various people: warriors, civil dignitaries, burghers, peasants. Some women and couples embracing are seen in the background. Frame. Frescoes: left, two men are embracing; right, two young men are standing on a boat, one of them punting and clasped in the arms of the other; below, a man seems to be inviting a king seated on a throne to mount a horse.

Just as the pomegranate contains many seeds in the same fruit, the king creates unity among the diverse social classes of the society of his realm. The Roman and "Gallic" costumes suggest that this scene could also be a historical allusion to the unification of Gaul by Caesar, and François I would thus appear as Caesar's successor. The side paintings seem to be a commentary on the idea of unity, whereas the scene below remains obscure. Some have interpreted it as being the announcement to Caesar of the rebellion of Vercingétorix. Others have wondered whether Rosso's original idea was to present the king as the Gallic chieftain Vercingétorix, the first to unite the Gallic tribes.

• *Third north bay*:
The Fire (fig. 121).
Main picture. People are fleeing from a town in flames situated on a rock by the sea. In the foreground two youths are carrying their aged parents on their backs, accompanied by children. Frame. Stuccoes: left, statue of a bearded man wearing breeches; right, statue of a young man, clad only in a loin-cloth. Fresco: below, a town on fire.

The scene was first considered to represent the burning of Troy and the flight of Aeneas, then it was thought to be the story of the twins who saved their parents from burning Catana following an eruption of Etna, in other words symbolising filial piety. The town in flames below could also represent Catana. As for the two stucco figures, could one be a Roman and the other a Gaul? If this picture is connected to the life of François I, it could evoke the devotion of the King's two sons, François and Henri, sent as hostages to Madrid in 1526, to allow the liberation of their father held prisoner since his defeat at Pavia.

90

• *Third south bay*: *Cleobis and Biton*.
Main picture. Cleobis and Biton have harnessed themselves to the chariot of their mother, Cydippe, priestess of Juno, and are leading her to the goddess's temple, one day when the oxen which were usually employed had not returned from the fields, having been struck down by the plague. Frame. Stuccoes: in bas-relief on the right, Cydippe in the midst of men and animals afflicted by the plague; left, the death of Cleobis and Biton; below, the episode known as Roman Charity: Pero succours her aged father Cimon at her breast, when he is imprisoned and condemned to die of hunger.

This picture expresses filial piety. It is generally thought to be an allusion to the great affection François I and his sister, Marguerite de Navarre, had for their mother, Louise de Savoie. It could also allude to the service of Divinity.

• *Fourth north bay*
Main picture: *The Nymph of Fontainebleau* (fig. 122) drawn by Couder (*c.* 1847) and painted by Alaux in 1860-1861 from a 16th-century engraving executed by Pierre Milan and René Boyvin from a drawing by Rosso (fig. 123). Frame. Plasterwork: copied in 1786 from the stuccoes on the opposite panel (by Roland?). Paintings: children by Alaux.

122. Jean Alaux, *The Nymph of Fontainebleau*, mural painting and plasterwork.

123. *The Nymph of Fontainebleau*, engraving by Pierre Milan and René Boyvin, after Rosso.

124. Primaticcio, *Danaë*, fresco.

• *Fourth south bay*: *Danaë*.
Main picture by Primaticcio (fig. 124). Danaë is in prison, guarded by a slave woman, and is visited by Jupiter transformed into golden rain. Frame by Rosso. Stuccoes: to the right and left, three female terminal figures bear a basket of fruit on their head. Frescoes: above, Apollo's chariot and Diana's chariot; below, child singers and musicians.

• *Fifth north bay*:
The Shipwreck or the Revenge of Nauplius.
Main picture. On their return from the Trojan war, the Greeks were subjected to the wrath of the gods, for they had violated their temples and Ajax had raped Cassandra in the sanctuary of Athena. The Greek fleet was therefore shipwrecked off the coast of Cape Caphareus. Athena caused Ajax to be struck by lightning and his dead body thrown on to the rocks (left). Nauplius, who wanted to take revenge on his compatriots, especially Ulysses who had had his son Palamedes put to death, lit a light on the rocks near the coast to lure the ships and most of them foundered.

In the foreground Nauplius and his followers are seen killing all those attempting to reach the shore. Frame. Stuccoes: numerous small bas-reliefs and two empty niches. Frescoes: below, Neptune and Amymone, the parents of Nauplius.

Was Nauplius a traitor or an avenger? In any case, revenge like betrayal engenders misfortune and death. Betrayal also rouses divine wrath. This episode has been interpreted as an allusion to the betrayal by the Connétable Charles de Bourbon, the King's cousin, who passed into the service of Charles V and was killed during the siege of Rome in 1527.

• *Fifth south bay*:
The Death of Adonis.
Main picture (fig. 125). The Cupids and Oreades are preparing to lay out the body of Adonis (killed by a wild boar). Above, a cupid is flying away with his garments. On the right, in the clouds, Venus on her chariot is tearing her hair in despair. Beside her are Eros, Fortune with her wheel and a weathercock on her head, and Adversity repre-

sented by a bent old woman holding some hammers. Frame. Stuccoes: on the left is the chariot of Cybele, drawn by a lion and lioness. Venus had warned Adonis to beware of wild beasts and had told him the story of how Cybele had changed Hippomenes and Atalanta into a lion and a lioness for having profaned her temples; on the right, an orgiastic scene; below, a chariot race. Frescoes: above, male and female couples clasped in each other's arms; below a recumbent woman and a cupid holding a bearded mask, another woman embracing a fox.

This seems to be an emblem of death and misfortune. The funerary theme is apparently associated with that of violent ambiguous passion. Dishonest lust is mortal. This idea does not correspond to the thesis whereby this fresco could be an allusion to the death of the Dauphin François at the age of seventeen on August 10, 1536.

• *Sixth north bay*: *The Education of Achilles*. Main picture. Chiron the centaur is educating the child Achilles: he is teaching him fencing, swimming, lance-throwing, music (above to the right), hunting (extreme right). Frame. Fresco: right and left, giants are chained to trees. Stucco: below, a battle scene.

The panel is an allegory in praise of the best education. The fettered giants seem to provide a contrast highlighting the main subject (a lack of education means slavery?). Could the battle scene prefigure the fate of Achilles? Do the small accessories evoke the time when Achilles was disguised as a girl during his stay with Lycomedes? The underlying theme of human mortality no doubt transpires here. Chiron was born immortal. Seriously wounded, he could only die if Prometheus gave him the right to death. On the other hand, Achilles, who had been plunged in the waters of the Styx by his mother to make him invulnerable, was unable to remain immortal.

125.
Rosso,
The Death of Adonis, fresco.

125

93

• *Sixth south bay*:
Man loses
Perpetual Youth
(fig. 126).

Main picture. This illustrates a fable told by a writer of the 2nd century B.C., Nicander of Colophon. Men had received from Jupiter the gift of eternal youth, but too lazy to carry it, they put it on the back of a donkey. When the donkey wanted to quench its thirst, a snake guarding the brook would not let it do so unless in exchange it was given Youth. Ever since, serpents change their skin every year and always remain young, whereas men inevitably grow old. Above left, a crowd is praying for youth in front of an altar; on his arrival from Olympus Mercury announces that their wish shall be granted. In the foreground on the left, a group illustrates the state of youth. In the middle the serpent is preparing to ravish Youth from the back of

the donkey. On the right, a group of old men illustrate old age. In the background, two scenes of sacrifice. Frame. Frescoes: left, people are entering a temple while the chariot of the gods appears in the sky; on the right, several allegorical figures, an old hag on crutches, a woman with three heads surrounded by bees (Slander), a woman astride a fox (Deceit), an old man with donkey's ears, spectacles and a lantern (Spying). Below, two dogs are lying near a chameleon.

This is the inevitability of growing old. Despite his desire, man is not immortal.

• *Seventh north bay*:
Venus frustrated.

Main picture. Venus is bathing and stretching out her hand to Cupid who is lying asleep. On the edge of the basin a young girl, fully dressed, hands folded, looks the other

126.
Rosso,
*Perpetual Youth
lost by Men*,
fresco and
stucco.

way. Cupids are flying through the air: one holds a shield, another a lance, another a helmet. Below right, another cupid is holding a closed book. Frame. Stuccoes: a young man on the left, a young woman on the right. Beneath their feet, bas-reliefs: a naval battle (left); a cavalry attack (right). Fresco: below, view of Fontainebleau from the pond, around 1535-1540.

Here Venus is attempting to rouse the sleeping Cupid; Mars is leaving for the battlefield. The draped figure could be marital affection imploring the goddess to awaken Cupid so that he brings the hero home. This panel, like its pair opposite, probably means that the fatality of war comes to upset love and a happy life. The association of Fontainebleau and Venus at the fountain may express the King's regret at having to abandon this home. The stucco couple could be an allegory of beauty and love.

• *Seventh south bay*:
The Battle of the Centaurs and the Lapiths.
Main picture. The drunken Centaurs are attacking the Lapiths on the wedding day of Pirithous and Hippodamia. The Lapiths win the combat. Frame. Stuccoes: on either side, mitred priests at the head of terms are holding on the left the royal F and on the right, the salamander; below, allegory of the causes of war. A man is standing, holding in front of him a mask (Cunning); behind appear Envy and Adversity. Another man is wallowing amidst the pigs (Intractability); the bear symbolises Anger, the wild boar Fury, the donkey Stupidity and Obstinacy. Frescoes: above, two recumbent men are blowing a trumpet decked with oriflammes bearing the royal salamander and fleurs-de-lis; below, children are playing equivocal games.

The panel illustrates War. Should it be seen as an allusion to the struggles with the House of Austria? The presence of trumpet-players suggests that it refers to the military victories of François I. As for the priests, does piety procure victory?

• *East end.*
Decorated in 1757. Putti in plasterwork, holding François I's F monogram, are due to the sculptor Jacques Verberckt. Bust of François I by Achille-Joseph Valois (1835).

Furniture: armchair (fig. 127) and table in Renaissance style, made by Grohé from designs by the architect Ruprich-Robert, 1862. Twenty-eight chairs with the salamander motif; twenty-two are the originals made by Jacob Frères and modified in 1862 by Steiner and Devineau, the other six are recent (1863).

Letter-box held by two greyhounds, due to Grohé, from models made by the sculptor Pierre-Louis Rouillard, 1868-1869. Chandeliers in the Renaissance style, Marquis, 1855.

127.
Armchair in walnut, made by Grohé for the François I Gallery in 1862.

Passage between the François I Gallery and the Guardroom

This passage was opened up in 1845 by Louis-Philippe to obtain direct access from one room to the other without having to go through the Saint Louis chambers. It was decorated with 17th-century pictures: French school, *Cupids on Clouds*; N. Coypel, *Equity*; also by Coypel, *Vigilance* (from the Tuileries); Damoiselet, *Cupid holding Flowers*; also by Damoiselet, *Cupid pressing Grapes* (from Marly); M. Corneille, *Morning*; also by Corneille, *Evening* (from Trianon).

To enter the Rotunda, one crosses the Guardroom (visited on the way back).

Rotunda

Decorated in 1836.

Nature, a marble statue by Niccolo Pericoli, known as Tribolo (*c.* 1500-1550), commissioned for François I in 1529, as a support for a basin which he had placed at Fontainebleau.

Standing lamp in Renaissance style, Chaumont, 1840.

Madame d'Etampes' bedroom, or the King's staircase (fig. 128)

During the reign of François I, this was the bedroom of his favourite, Madame d'Etampes. In the 17th century, it was the Alexander Chamber, then the antechamber of Madame de Maintenon's apartment. In 1749 it became the King's staircase.

History: this room was embellished between 1541 and 1544 by Primaticcio. The whole decoration of the west wall (on the guard-room side) dates from this time and it was perhaps then that the general distribution of the stuccowork on all four sides was carried

128. La chambre de la duchesse d'Étampes ou escalier du Roi.
128. Bedchamber of the Duchesse d'Etampes or the King's staircase.

out. It is not known however whether this room was then lit by two or four windows in the north and south walls, or how many frescoes there were altogether, or even what the ceiling and panelling looked like. The story of Alexander was not chosen at random to decorate the royal favourite's bedroom. The three frescoes extant on the west side show that Primaticcio treated the subject in his usual measured and elegant style. In *The Marriage of Alexander and Roxana*, he followed faithfully a composition deriving from Raphael's atelier. As for the stucco frames, the rhythm is imposed by the great elonga-

ted female figures, highly Mannerist, in which the influence of Parmigianino is apparent. Strapwork motifs, putti, bunches of fruit, heads of he-goats and satyr terms are all present. In 1570 Nicolo dell'Abbate was given the task of producing new frescoes. This was no doubt due to the fact that the Fine Chimney wing which had just been erected overshadowed the south wall. Indeed, Nicolo's colours are found in both frescoes on this side. However, according to a remark made by Mme S. Béguin, historian of the Fontainebleau School, the subject on the left, representing a woman stepping into Alexan-

der's bed, is too free to have been accepted by Catherine de Médicis who was anxious to set heroic examples for her son Charles IX. It is most likely therefore that Nicolo merely restored a subject painted thirty years earlier and that only one single window was blocked up by the new construction. A third alteration was made to the decoration in 1748-1749 when Louis XV ordered a staircase to be built on this spot leading to his apartment. Although the King had decided to keep the former decoration, the east wall had to be rebuilt and so the stucco work adorning it had to be removed. The sculptor Verberckt and his team put them back again but were unable to save the frescoes. The wrought-iron banisters, from a design of Gabriel, were then produced by the locksmith Parent. The final important transformation occurred in 1834 under Louis-Philippe. As always, the king was not content to refurbish, preferring to create afresh. The painter Abel de Pujol restored the 16th-century frescoes, completed the mural decoration with three new compositions and had a painting on canvas made for the ceiling, representing *The Apotheosis of Alexander* (1834-1836). Regarding the east wall, he sought inspiration among the prints after Primaticcio referring to Alexander, which were supposed to have been painted in this room. The ceiling was raised and, in order to decorate the new voussoir in the Renaissance fashion, he called in the sculptor Huber who employed carton pierre, and the painter Moench (1836-1837); it is decorated with bronze camaieu portraits resembling medals, representing Louis VII and Louis IX, François I and Henri II, Henri IV and Louis XIII, Louis XVI and Napoléon. The portraits of Louis-Philippe and Marie-Amélie which accompanied them disappeared after 1848. This room was restored from 1962 to 1964 by MM. Binnenbaum and Ledeur.

Description of the mural decoration: west wall by Primaticcio, *circa* 1541-1544. Medallion above the entrance door: *Alexander breaking in Bucephalus* (fig. 129). Large picture: *The Marriage of Alexander and Roxana*. Second medallion: *Alexander sparing Timoclea, a Theban Woman*. South wall. Right: *Alexander stows Homer's Works into a Casket*, by Nicolo dell'Abbate, 1570. Left: *Thalestris (?) climbing into Alexander's Bed*, by Nicolo dell'Abbate, 1570? East wall by Abel de Pujol, 1834-1835. End medallion: *Alexander cutting the Gordian Knot*. Large picture: *The Banquet at Persepolis*, from an engraving by D. Florentin. Medallion above the door: *Alexander and Campaspe* painted by Apelles, from an engraving by L. Davent (repainted in its original place).

Furniture: gilt bronze brackets for a carcel lamp, Chaumont, 1838. Two candelabra in Sarreguemines faience, First Empire (entered in 1860). Two benches in painted wood, Quignon, Second Empire, covered with an 18th-century Savonnerie carpet (entered in 1863).

129.
Primaticcio,
Alexander breaking in Bucephalus,
fresco surrounded by stucco
caryatids and putti.

Salle de bal (fig. 130)

"Salle du bal"(ballroom) or "grande salle du bal" (large ballroom). From 1664, the Swiss, or Hundred-Swiss, Guardroom (until the Revolution). 1810, banqueting hall. From *circa* 1820, Henri II Gallery.

History: the building in which the ballroom is situated, erected in the reign of François I by the contractor Gilles Le Breton, was to have a loggia in the Italian style on the first floor covered by a vaulted roof, which explains the presence on the piles of consoles intended to receive the springs of the arches. Unfinished when the King died, the project was resumed in Henri II's day and transformed by the architect Philibert Delorme. In 1548 the storeys were divided up. In 1550 Delorme contracted the joiner Francisque Scibec de Carpi, who had already worked in the François I Gallery, to take charge of all the woodwork: in February, the floor, the platform in front of the fireplace and the windows; in June, the ceiling, the musicians' gallery and the wainscotting. The mural decoration is thought to have followed in the 1550s. Primaticcio was responsible for the

130. The ballroom.

preparatory drawings and Nicolo dell'Abbate with his team of assistants successfully carried out the frescoes. We know that the monumental chimneypiece (created by Delorme, using two of the bronze statues cast by Primaticcio at Fontainebleau itself) was painted and gilded in 1556. As for the carved stone door at the entrance to the room, it probably dates back to the end of Henri II's reign (a contract was signed for the gilding in 1558 and the wooden doors were made by Perret). According to Abbé Guilbert, in Henri IV's reign the frescoes already needed restoring and Toussaint Dubreuil

was probably commissioned to do so. In 1642 the Surintendant Sublet de Noyers asked Poussin to find a way to prevent deterioration. However, as the room no longer served for balls in Louis XIV's reign, no one cared about the condition it was in. During the Revolution the two bronze satyrs from the chimney were removed to recuperate the metal and Napoléon was obliged to replace them in 1805 by two plaster columns designed by Percier and Fontaine. Thirty years later, the revival of interest in monuments of the past incited Louis-Philippe to have the room completely refurbished. He entrusted Jean Alaux, in 1834, with the task of restoring the frescoes, employing the Vivet encaustic wax method, an operation which entailed completing and repainting them entirely. The Parisian joiner Poncet, with the help of the sculptor Lambert-Théophile Lefébure, restored the ceiling and the gallery, redid the panelling and laid a new parquet floor matching the coffered pattern of the ceiling (1835-1836). The decoration was finally enhanced with some new door and window fastenings (Mignon), but the two columns of 1805 were kept. In the second half of the 19th century, the frescoes again needed repairing (in 1858, 1865, 1883-1885). In 1963-1966 they were once more restored, but the results could only be unsatisfactory, owing to the poor state of the old frescoes. Attempts were made to remove Alaux's handiwork, but it proved necessary to maintain many of his contributions to avoid leaving gaps (restorers: M. Binenbaum and Mlle Pector). The two bronze satyrs from the chimneypiece were recast in Rome, employing new moulds taken from antique statues at the Capitole Museum. The 19th-century panelling was recarved using a pattern from the old 16th-century panels and lastly, the bay was reopened in the gallery and painted helmets were removed from the frieze below, though, as documents prove, they were prior to the 19th century. In 1985 a dais in front of the chimney was reconstituted like the one which stood there in the 17th century.

Emblems: the emblems of Henri II are scattered all over the room: the coat-of-arms of France and the collar of the Order of Saint

Michael; the letter H, sometimes associated with another letter which could be C (Catherine de Médicis, the Queen) or D (Diane de Poitiers, the King's mistress); the emblem of the sovereign and Diana, the crescent moon (alone or intertwined in groups of three); the royal motto: *Donec totum impleat orbem* (until it [the crescent] has filled the whole disk, i.e. until the King has filled the whole world with the glory of his name). On the chimneypiece there are also bows, arrows and quivers, other emblems of the King and of Diane de Poitiers.

Description of the mural decoration: this consists of mythological scenes and characters, as well as allegorical figures, but the order in which they appear and their meaning is not always clear.

• *Chimney wall*: allegories of Diana and Hunting. Above left, a gentleman who appears to be Sebastien de Rabutin killing a lynx, an episode which was said to have occurred in the forest of Fontainebleau in 1548 (fig. 131); below, Diana with the Dog Cerberus (effaced) and Cupid. Above right, Hercules and the Wild Boar of Erymanthus; below, Diana in a Chariot drawn by Dragons.

• *Side walls*:
1° Large paintings between the arches. Oval Courtyard side (starting from the entrance door): Feast of Bacchus; Apollo and the Muses at Parnassus; The Three Graces dancing before the Gods (fig. 132); The Wedding Feast of Thetis and Peleus and the Apple of Discord. On the garden side (starting from the chimney): Jupiter and Mercury in the Dwelling of Philemon and Baucis; Phaeton imploring the Sun to allow him to drive his Chariot; Vulcan forging the Arms Venus wants for Cupid (fig. 133); The Harvest. Beneath the eight carved corbels, arms trophies.

2° Subjects of the paintings in the window recesses. Oval Courtyard side. *First window* (from left to right): The Ocean (?); Man with a Child holding Fruit; Cupid in the Air; Woman holding an Oar, A Child and a Man wreathed with Vine Shoots; Nymph (or a Spring). *Second window*: Jupiter; Two Men at the Helm; Mars; Two Men; Juno. *Third window*: Pan; Two Men, One holding a Torch; Pomona (?): Æsculapius (?) and another Man, a Serpent and a Stick beside Them; Abundance. *Fourth window*: Hercules; Charon, another Man and Cerberus the Dog; Man asleep; Saturn and Mercury; Dejanira holding the Tunic of Nessus. *Fifth window*: Adonis (?); Two Men leaning (Advice?); Cupid in the Air; Recumbent Woman and a Cock (Vigilance?); Venus adorned with the Weapons of Mars.

Garden side. *Fifth window* (close to the chimney): Venus and Cupid; Narcissus; Ganymede abducted by Jupiter changed into an Eagle; Wounded Female Warrior (Amazon?) and Woman holding an Arrow; Mars (?). *Fourth window*: Amphitrite; Arion;

131.
Primaticcio (after),
Sébastien de Rabutin killing a Loup-cervier in the Forest of Fontainebleau in 1548,
fresco.

Vulcan (?) holding a Net; Two Men with a Lion (Assurance?); Neptune. *Third window*: Woman holding a Bowl (Hebe?); Two Men (Resolution?); Janus; A Spring and another Woman; Bacchus (?); *Second window*: Cybele; Mars and Venus; Night (or Truth) holding a Torch; Cupid, Eros and a Man lamenting; Saturn. *First window*: Flora (?); Two Men asleep beside Poppies (Sleep?); Man seated on a Cathedra; Two Men near a Fire (Winter?); Vulcan (?).
• *End wall*: above the gallery, A Concert.

Furniture: chandeliers in Renaissance style, Soyer et Ingé, 1837. Fire-dogs in Renaissance style, Chaumont, 1836.

132. Primaticcio (after), *The Three Graces dancing before the Gods*, fresco.
133. Primaticcio (after), *Vulcan's Forge*, fresco.

Apartment of Madame de Maintenon

None of the 16th-century occupants of this apartment are known. In 1625, the Princesse de Conti, Louise-Marguerite de Lorraine, daughter of Henri de Guise, the Balafré (the Scarred one); in 1641, the famous Marquis de Cinq-Mars, Master of the Horse and the King's favourite (who was decapitated in 1642); in Louis XIV's reign, the Maréchal de Villeroy († 1685), then Madame de Maintenon from 1686 until the King's death, all lodged here. In the reign of Louis XV, the apartment was allotted to the Duchesse de Bourbon, daughter of Louis XIV and Madame de Montespan († 1743), then to the Duchess of Modena, Charlotte-Aglaé d'Orléans († 1761), daughter of the Regent and finally to the Comte de la Marche and his wife Marie-Fortunée d'Este, daughter of Charlotte-Aglaé d'Orléans.

In 1804, Prince Louis, the Emperor's brother, lived here; in 1837, at the wedding of the Duc d'Orléans, it was occupied by the Duc and Duchesse de Broglie; in 1839 by the Maréchal Gérard; from 1845 onwards, by Madame Adélaïde, the King's sister. In Napoléon III's time, this was the apartment of Princesse Mathilde, but in 1863 and 1864 Princesse Anna Murat (future Duchesse de Mouchy) lodged here and in 1868, the Duc d'Albe, the Empress's brother-in-law.

Passage

Formerly a washroom installed in 1835-1836 by Louis-Philippe in place of a terrace. In the 20th century it lost its 19th-century aspect.

Bedroom

(fig. 134)

Decoration: woodwork of the early 18th century (c. 1725), enriched by Louis-Philippe.

Furniture: as it was in Louis-Philippe's day. Bed in gilded wood for Madame Élisabeth at Fontainebleau, by Sené et Vallois, under the direction of Hauré, 1787. Two armchairs (fig. 135) and a "spur" footstool (fig. 136) which belonged to Marie-Antoinette at Saint-Cloud, 1787. In 1837 this furniture was upholstered in white satin with a green diamond-shaped pattern and bouquets of flowers, woven in 1812-1814 by Lacostat in Lyon for Versailles, with a border woven for Meudon in 1809-1810. All this material was rewoven in 1979-1982. The alcove hangings, the drapery round the bed and the glass-panelled door were remade in 1981-1983. Chest-of-drawers with Boulle marquetry, late 17th to early 18th century (purchased from Baron in 1837). The Three Graces clock with a Lepaute movement, circa 1770 (entered in 1804), had belonged to General Moreau. Louis-XVI candelabra (same origin). Louis-XVI fire-dogs (entered in 1835).

Cabinet

Decoration: wood panelling, 1686 (by Lalande). Louis-XV mantlepiece placed in 1836.

Furniture: Second Empire. Armchairs in gilded wood, stamped Sené (entered in 1837) covered with the same material as the one in the preceding room. Curtains remade in 1981-1983. Low cupboard, part 18th-century, made from a former corner cupboard transformed in the 19th century (bought from Benoit, 1856). Pier table in the Louis-XV style (entered in 1863). 18th-century Boulle marquetry clock (bought from Delaunai, 1836). Louis-XVI Sèvres bottle-shaped vases. Louis-XVI wall-lights (entered in 1857). Louis-XVI fire-dogs (entered in 1835). Two Second Empire Beauvais tapestry pictures: *Spring* and *Jewels* (signed A. Milice).

134.
Bedchamber
in Madame de Maintenon's
apartment, as it was in
Louis-Philippe's time (reconstituted).

135.
Sené and Vallois, armchair from
Marie-Antoinette's cabinet interieur
at Saint-Cloud, 1787.

136.
Sené and Vallois, "spur" stool,
same provenance.

Loggia and large drawing-room (fig. 137)

Decoration: the large bay of the 16th-century loggia was glazed in 1641 to make the apartment more comfortable, but the woodwork decorating it dates from 1686. The present stained glass was recently reconstituted (1983) as it was in Louis XIV's reign. The drawing-room was Madame de Maintenon's bedchamber. The mural decoration was done partly in 1686 (wood panelling and pier glass with cupids and the royal sun, facing the chimney; cornucopia around the medallions at the top of the walls) and partly in 1836 (pier glass above the mantlepiece, panels bearing coats-of-arms and rosettes in carton pierre, installation of the Louis-XVI chimney).

Furniture: as it was in the Second Empire. In the loggia, 18th-century chandelier, enlarged in 1847. Louis-XVI painted wooden stools. In the drawing-room, an important set of seats in gilded wood in the Louis-XIV style covered with petit-point tapestry dating from the late 17th century (entered in 1863), after having been at the Tuileries. The sofa

and armchairs were bought in 1855, at the Exposition universelle, from the upholstery firm Mégard et Duval which had furnished without cost a rest room for the Empress on the first floor of the Palais de l'Industrie. The chairs were made at the Garde-Meuble; they were gilded by Mars and covered with tapestry panels which came from the same upholsterers as the window lambrequin. It is worth noting that the cover of the sofa was also cut out of panels of wall hangings, whereas the covers of the armchairs were originally made especially for seats. The so-called "Mazarin" desk in Boulle marquetry is from the end of the 17th century; it was restored in the 19th century (bought from Maury, Combes et Cie, 1835). Pier table in gilt wood, early 18th century (bought from Soliliage Jeune, 1837). 18th-century chandelier, enlarged in 1847. Four wall-lights in the Louis-XIV style, no doubt by Chaumont, made at the time of Louis-Philippe. White marble clock representing Innocence teased by Cupid, Furet movement, reign of Louis XVI. Fire-dogs in gilt bronze, Louis XVI (entered in 1804). Two pairs of Sèvres vases with a pink ground, one pair baluster-shaped, copied in 1858 from some "Grec à

137. Large drawing-room in Madame de Maintenon's apartment.

rosaces" vases made in the reign of Louis XVI, the other with medallions depicting 17th-century noblewomen, 1859 (both pairs entered in 1863).

Antechamber

Bathroom in the 18th century. Antechamber since the 19th century.

Decoration: Louis-XV panelling.

Furniture: as at the end of the 19th century. Painted wooden chairs upholstered in Beauvais tapestry, First Empire (entered in 1832). Marquetry commode, Louis XVI's reign. Wall-lights (bought from Duverger, 1804). Clock, Cupid, Lepaute movement, *circa* 1765-1770 (entered in 1804). Fire-dogs (bought from Ravrio, 1809). Two carafe vases, Sèvres manufactory, 1857.

Passage

Lantern shaped like a *cul-de-lampe*, in crystal, First Empire (entered in 1835).

Vestibule of Madame de Maintenon's apartment

Decoration: woodwork, 1834.

Sculpture: J. Debay, *Modesty gives in to Love* (Salon of 1853).

Pictures: they were part of the decoration of the Château, since vanished or transformed, or they evoke it by copies: Primaticcio (after), *Menelaus in Despair* (subject depicted in Charles IX's bedchamber); Franco-Flemish School at the beginning of the 17th century, two landscapes (taken from Henri IV's Hunts apartment in the keeper's lodge at the Château); A. Dubois, *Allegory of Painting and Sculpture* (from the former Aviary Room) and also *Allegory of the Marriage of Henri IV and Marie de Médicis* (fig. 138); after the same artist, *Flora* (subject depicted in 1642 in the King's bedchamber); J. Dubois (after), *Felicity* with the features of

138. Ambroise Dubois,
Allegory of the Marriage of Henri IV and Marie de Médicis.

Anne d'Autriche (subject painted in 1642 for the Queen's bedchamber at Fontainebleau, original in the Louvre).

Furniture: late 18th-century lantern (entered in 1810). Bracket for two carcel lamps, Chaumont, 1841.

Antechamber of the former theatre, called the Louis XV small drawing-room

Decorated in 1840. On the ceiling: M.A. Challe, *The Alliance of Painting and Sculpture* (Salon of 1753). On the walls: 17th-century French School, *Allegorical Figure*: F. Verdier, seven figures of gods holding the signs of the Zodiac illustrating the months: Minerva (Ram, March), Venus (Bull, April), Jupiter (Lion, July), Ceres (Virgin, August), Vulcan (Balance, September), Diana (Archer, November), Vesta (Goat, December), cartoons painted around 1685-1696 after 16th-century tapestries called The Months with grotesques or "grotesques de Guise", which served as patterns when they were rewoven at the Gobelins factory.

Brackets for a carcel lamp, Chaumont, 1838 (identical to those on the King's staircase).

140.
Chimney
in the guardroom.

Sovereigns' state apartments

Guardroom (fig. 139)

Created around 1570. In the 17th and 18th centuries, the King's Guardroom. 1804, Emperor's antechamber. 1814, King's antechamber. 1837, Guardroom.

Decoration: ceiling and frieze at the top of the walls attributed to Ruggiero de Ruggieri *circa* 1570, rearranged in Louis XIII's day. Mural decoration in Renaissance style painted by Charles Moench, 1834-1836; it is devoted to historic figures: their portraits, coats-of-arms, monograms, together with those of their wives and their emblems and devices, accompanied by allegorical figures: François I and Henri II (wall of the first Saint Louis Chamber); Antoine de Bourbon, Duc de Vendôme, father of Henri IV, and Marie de Médicis (chimney wall); Henri IV and Louis XIII (wall at right angles); Anne d'Autriche, then the salamander of Fran-

çois I which has replaced the portrait of Louis-Philippe (window wall). Marble chimney (fig. 140) assembling fragments of sculpture of different origins: large frame adorned with allegories of the seasons and the elements, carved in 1555-1556 by Pierre Bontemps for Henri II's bedchamber in the Stove Pavilion; two tall figures of *Force* (in fact representing *Clemency*) and *Peace* by Mathieu Jacquet (1600-1601) from Henri IV's Fine Chimney; bust of Henri IV also attributed to Jacquet, from the former aviary; the rest of the chimneypiece was sculpted by Jean-Baptiste-Louis Plantar, 1836. Parquet floor of diverse woods, Poncet, 1837.

Furniture: as it was in the Second Empire. Folding stools in gilded wood, Rode, 1806, for the Empress's first reception room. Louis-XIV screen in gilded wood (bought from Laflèche, 1835). Dining-table, *circa*

139. Guardroom.

1800, from the Paris residence of General Moreau. Chandeliers in gilt bronze, Boulle style, Chaumont (Exposition des Produits de l'Industrie française, 1834). Nine wall-lights in the same style, Chaumont, 1837. Sèvres porcelain Renaissance vase "in the style of Bernard Palissy", from a design by Aimé Chenavard, 1832. Fire-dogs in gilt bronze, 17th-century style (bought from Recappé, 1866).

First Saint Louis Chamber

The King's reception room, then an ante-chamber (called the Buffet Room in the 18th century because the buffet was set up here for the King). From 1757, it was joined to the following room to form the King's first ante-chamber. 1807, Pages Room. 1814, Guard-room. 1837, the first Saint Louis Chamber.

Decoration: work took place in 1757: arcade, wood panelling, coffered ceiling. Further operations in 1836: gilded carton-pierre ornamentation on the ceiling, executed by Huber on Louis-XIV models at the Château de Versailles; various pictures hang here: five come from two other rooms in the Château, the Oval Chamber *(Story of Theagenes and Chariclea*, see p.112 below) and the queen's former cabinet *(Story of Tancred and Clorinda*, see p.122 below), painted by Ambroise Dubois in the early 17th century (from left to right, starting at the first window: 1. *Chariclea taking Care of Theagenes wounded* [scene 12]; 2. *Tancred and the Crusaders before the Walls of Jerusalem*; 3. *First Meeting of Theagenes and Chariclea* [scene 2]; 4. *Procession of Chariclea during the Pythian Games* [scene 1]; 5. *Clorinda before Aladin*; two allegories, *Hope* and *Faith*, 17th-century French school; four pictures of children, from Marly, painted by Florentin Damoiselet and Pierre Poisson in 1684-1686.

Furniture: as in the Second Empire. Seats in black wood in the Louis-XIV style, carved by Fourdinois, upholstered with a Savonnerie carpet with a blue ground adorned with bouquets of flowers, woven from cartoons by

141.
Clock,
Apollo's Chariot.

Chabal-Dussurgey and Godefroy. Large clock attributed to Boulle et Fils, *circa* 1725, decorated with a group of Apollo's Chariot, inspired by the one on Apollo's Basin at Versailles (fig. 141). This clock belonged to the Château de Chantilly in 1740. Sent during the Directoire to the Palais du Luxembourg, it had been given in 1835 by the Chambre des Pairs (Upper House of Parliament) to Louis-Philippe and was installed here in 1837. Two writing tables in the Boulle style, Alphonse Jacob-Desmalter, 1840. Chandeliers, Chaumont (Exposition des Produits de l'Industrie française, 1834). Wall-lights, Chaumont, 1837.

Second Saint Louis Chamber

From the Middle Ages to the end of the 16th century, the King's bedchamber. In the 17th and 18th centuries, the King's antechamber, then, from 1737, the King's first antechamber, called Saint Louis's chamber or bedchamber and sometimes the dining-room, for the King was in the habit of taking meals here. 1804, room for the Officers of the Emperor's Household. 1814, Saint Louis Chamber. 1837, second Saint Louis Chamber.

Decoration: work was undertaken in 1757: arcade, wood panelling, coffered ceiling, mantlepiece in Languedoc marble. More work in 1836: the ceiling embellished as in the preceding room and framework of the famous bas-relief of Henri IV on horseback from the Fine Chimney (Mathieu Jacquet, 1600-1601) (fig. 142); ancient pictures were then hung, five scenes from the life of Henri IV painted by Vincent in 1783-1787, to serve as cartoons for Gobelin tapestries; *Gabrielle d'Estrées fainting* (left of the arcade); *Henri IV raising Sully prostrate at his Feet in Fontainebleau*; *Henri IV having Supper with Michaut the Miller at Lieusaint*; *Henri IV encountering Sully wounded* (facing the windows); *Henri IV taking Leave of Gabrielle d'Estrées on his Departure to join his Army* (right of the chimney) and ten pictures of children which had been part of the decoration at Marly (see the first Saint Louis Chamber).

Furniture: as in the Second Empire. Same set of chairs, chandeliers and sconces as in the preceding room. Patinated bronze fire-dogs representing Venus and Adonis, from Renaissance models (bought from Bruant, 1860).

Passage

On the ceiling, *Three Cupids on Clouds*, 17th-century French school.

142.
Mathieu Jacquet,
*Henri IV
on horseback*,
marble bas-relief.

Louis XIII Chamber (fig. 143)

Since the beginning of the 17th century, the King's great cabinet, called the Oval Chamber. From 1737, served as the King's second antechamber, but was usually called the Theagenes Chamber. Like the antechamber at Versailles, sometimes it was also called *Oeil-de-Boeuf*. 1804, High Dignitaries Chamber. 1814, Noblemen's Chamber. 1837, Louis XIII Chamber.

Decoration: ceiling and walls, early 17th century (around 1610, the date appearing on the beams), except for the great doors pierced in the original decor, 1757. Paintings by Ambroise Dubois (*c.* 1543-1614) depicting the romance between Theagenes and Chariclea from the Greek novel written in the 4th century A.D. by Heliodorus of Emesa and translated in the 16th century by Amyot (eleven paintings are still *in situ*, three others are in the first Saint Louis Chamber: in the

order in which the story unfolds, taking into account the fact that scenes 1, 2 and 12 are in the first Saint Louis Chamber], *The Sacrifice of Theagenes and the Thessalians at Delphi* [scene 3] on the fireplace; *Calasiris's Dream* [scene 4] (fig. 144), *Ailing Chariclea examined by Doctor Acestinus* [scene 5]; *Meeting between Calasiris and Chariclea* [scene 6] on the ceiling; *Chariclea abducted by Theagenes* [scene 7] on the wall to the left of the entrance; *Vow of Theagenes* [scene 8] in the centre of the ceiling; *Theagenes, Chariclea and Calasiris embark on their Return to Egypt* [scene 9] on the wall after scene 7; *Chariclea with Theagenes wounded on the Shores of Egypt* [scene 11] on the left of the chimney; *Theagenes and Chariclea taken Prisoner by Brigands on the Isle of Shepherds* [scene 13] on the wall opposite the windows; *Theagenes returns to the Isle of Shepherds in Search of Chariclea* [scene 14] and *Theagenes finds Chariclea in a Cave* [scene 15], on the ceiling on the

143. Louis XIII Chamber.

window side. Also on the ceiling, painted by Dubois on plaster, *Crowning of the Dauphin Louis* with, on the left, *Apollo and Diana* (?), on the right, *Hercules and Dejanira*.

The mural decoration (fig. 145) consists of landscapes and multicoloured bouquets, scenes and figures in grisaille, flowers on a gold ground. The monograms scattered all over the decoration are those of Henri IV and Marie de Médicis, Louis XIII, as Dauphin and as King, and of his brother the Duc d'Orléans, as well as the crossed S, a cryptic sign often used by Henri IV which signifies constancy and steadfastness (fig. 146).

The mirror set in the wood panelling was installed by the architect Duban in 1849 as a reminder of the first mirror to be imported from Venice into France which, according to legend, Henri IV had placed here.

144.
Ambroise Dubois,
The Dream of Calasiris (Story of Theagenes and Chariclea).

145.
Louis XIII Chamber, detail of the painted wood panelling.

146.
Louis XIII Chamber, detail of the painted wood panelling: the barred S and the initial M.

Furniture: as at the time of the Second Empire (except for the carpet and the comfortable armchairs which are missing). Louis-XIV seats, some of them 17th-century (a settee, ten armchairs, a footstool, bought at the sale of the Château d'Effiat in 1856) and the others made in 1857 (a settee, eight chairs, a footstool made in the cabinet-makers' workshop at the Mobilier de la Couronne). They are upholstered in blue damask (rewoven in 1958). Light chairs in gilded wood, bought from Souty, gilder, 1858. Six white "Chiavari" chairs, by G. Descalzi, known as Campanino & Sons, cabinet-makers at Chiavari, Italy. Carved beechwood table, Fourdinois, 1860. Family table, Boulle style, A. Jacob-Desmalter, 1840. 17th-century pier table in gilded wood (bought from Chapsal in 1835). Gilt paste pier table in the Louis-XIV style, Servais, gilder (Exposition des Produits de l'Industrie française, 1839). Ivory chest, Germany, first half of the 17th century. Chandeliers, 18th century. Eleven wall-lights, Renaissance style, Chaumont, 1837. Vermeil desk-lamp, Biennais, 1809. Fire-dogs with young tritons, Chaumont, 1836. Bronze group *Catching the Fox. Hunting in Scotland* by P.J. Mène, 1861 (fig. 147). Chalice-shaped vase in painted enamel, *The Seasons*, by Gobert, Sèvres factory, Second Empire.

François I Chamber

Probably the Queen's bedchamber from 1531 onwards. Became an antechamber after the new suite of rooms was built overlooking the Diana Garden; it served in the 17th and 18th centuries as the Queen's Public Dining-room (*Grand Couvert de la Reine*). 1804, dining-room. 1837, François I Chamber.

Decoration: chimney (fig. 148) adorned with stuccowork and frescoes by Primaticcio between 1534 and 1537 (the principal medallion represents *The Marriage of Venus and Adonis*, from a drawing by Jules Romain). Ceiling, 16th century (restored in the 19th century). Low wainscoting decorated with the monogram and emblem of Anne d'Autriche (the pelican), *circa* 1644. Overdoor by Blanchin, 1861.

Furniture: as in the Second Empire, but the greater part was reconstituted in 1979. Tapestries of the *Hunts of Maximilian* after Van Orley, Gobelins, late 17th century to early 18th century. Seats in gilded wood in the Louis-XIV style, covered in Beauvais tapestry with a "Byzantine pattern" on a pink ground, delivered in 1852; the woodwork, identical to that of the black seats in the Saint Louis Chambers, can be attributed to

149

147

147.
P.J. Mène,
Catching a Fox, Hunting in Scotland,
bronze group.

148.
Chimney in the François I Chamber.

149.
Odyssey Cabinet, carved ebony,
mid-17th century.

Fourdinois. Cabinet known as the Odyssey Cabinet (fig. 149), owing to its interior decoration executed from engravings by Van Tulden of scenes in the former Ulysses Gallery at Fontainebleau, carved ebony, first half of the 17th century (bought from M. de Blesbourg and Mme de Nollent, 1826). Cabinet called the Caryatid Cabinet, carved ebony, first half of the 17th century and 19th century (purchased from Noël Picot, 1835; altered in 1862). Two cupboards in Boulle style, A. Jacob-Desmalter, 1839. Table in gilded wood, Louis-XIV style, by Cruchet, 1860, from designs by the architect Ruprich-Robert for the Apollo drawing-room at the Tuileries. Chandeliers, 18th century, seven wall-lights in Renaissance style, Chaumont, 1840. Chimera fire-dogs, Chaumont, 1837 (fig. 150). Bowl in porcelain from the Adolphe Hache et Pépin Le Halleur factory at Vierzon, Second Empire. Two red porphyry vases, Italy, 17th century (from Louis XIV's collection). Red porphyry vases mounted in gilt bronze, *circa* 1770 (purchased for Louis XVI in 1784 at the Montribloud sale). Vases in green marble mounted in gilt bronze, Louis-XVI period (former Egmont-Pignatelli collection). Savonnerie rug, Restoration period, woven for the Throne Room at the Tuileries from designs by Jean-Démosthène Dugourc in 1818 (only the sides of this carpet are seen here).

150.
Fire-iron with chimerae,
by Chaumont, delivered in 1837.

152.
Desk in Boule style by Alphonse
Jacob-Desmalter, delivered in 1840..

Tapestries Chamber (fig. 151)

In the 16th century, the Queen's bedchamber and then the Queen's guardroom. 1768, the Queen's first antechamber (it then acquired its present size). 1804, the Empress's first drawing-room. 1814, Queen's Guardroom. 1837, Tapestries Chamber.

Decoration: chimney, 1731. Ceiling in northern pine, Renaissance style, Poncet, 1835.

Furniture: as it was in the Second Empire, in course of reconstitution since 1979. Tapestries depicting the story of Psyche, Paris workshops, first half of the 17th century. Seats belonging to the set in the François I Chamber. Two large low cupboards in Boulle style, A. Jacob-Desmalter, 1839. Desk (fig. 152) and family table, A. Jacob-Desmalter, 1840. Savonnerie rug, Restoration period, woven for the blue drawing-room in the King's apartment at the Tuileries from the cartoon by Saint-Ange in 1817. 18th-century chandelier. Vase-shaped candelabra, Louis-XVI period (purchased from Legendre, 1804). Two pairs of candelabra in Louis-XVI style, Napoléon III period (bought from Hervoit, 1857). Gilt bronze fire-dogs, Louis-XVI period (purchased in 1804). Boulle mantle clock with movement due to Masson in Paris, 18th century (purchased at the Louis Fould sale, 1860). Pénicaud-type bowl, enamel by Gobert, Manufacture de Sèvres, Second Empire period.

151. Tapestries Chamber.

The Empress's Antechamber

Queen's Guardroom, created in 1768 in place of the former Queen's staircase, dating from the 16th century, and part of the preceding room. Since 1804, antechamber.

Decoration: ceiling and panelling, 1835.

Furniture: in 1979-1980 was refurnished as it had been during the Second Empire. Gobelins tapestries, *The Seasons*, after Le Brun (second set, 1673): *Summer, Autumn, Winter*. English-style seats, Second Empire, wood upholstered in green velvet, redone in 1980: two sofas, four chairs. The two armchairs are copies. Pier table and desk in carved oak, Fourdinois, 1865. Chandelier, 18th century. Two brackets for a carcel lamp, Chaumont, 1841, for the Fresco Gallery. Cartel clock in the Boulle style, surmounted by a figure of Fame (purchased from David, 1862). Two "Indian-type" enamel vases, Manufacture de Sèvres, Second Empire.

Cross the vestibule to reach the Diana Gallery.

The Diana Gallery
(fig. 153)

History: situated on the first floor of the brick and stone building erected in 1600 by Henri IV, this gallery belonged to the Queen's apartments. At that time it was painted under the direction of the Flemish artists Ambroise Dubois and Jean de Hoey and dedicated to the myth of Diana and to the victories of Henri IV. This decoration was ruined at the beginning of the 19th century when Napoléon decided to reconstruct the entire gallery (some fragments of the vaulted ceiling, saved from destruction, were put back in the Fresco or the Plates Gallery at the time of Louis-Philippe).

The architect Hurtault (1765-1824) was the author of the new project inspired by the ideas of Percier and Fontaine for the great gallery in the Louvre. From 1810 to 1814 the main constructions were completed

(vault, parquet floor, doors and windows), as well as the ornamental part of the decoration (columns, pilasters and stucco panels by Zobl; frieze carvings, capitals, window frames and door jambs, panelling by Mouret; window hasps by Forestier; picture frames by Morisot; column and pilaster bases in bronze by Delafontaine, decorative paintings on the vault by Moench: framework, tora with green and gold camaieu fruit, martial bas-reliefs in red camaieu, decorative paintings on the arched ceilings of the entrance hall and the room at the end, known then as the Roi de Rome's room, by Redouté). There was not enough time to carry out the whole iconographic programme decided by the Emperor, who wished to evoke different feats during his reign and, in the end room, allegories relating to the Roi de Rome (his son).

Before fixing a new programme, the Restoration began by asking Moench and Redouté to efface the various Napoleonic emblems scattered throughout the gallery. Work was not resumed until 1817. As a souvenir of the former decoration dating back to the reign of Henri IV (see above p.73), it was decided that the new one would be devoted to the myth of Diana; the end room to the "Chaste Goddess" and the arches of the gallery to the "Goddess of Hunting". As for the mural decoration of the gallery, since it was no longer possible to depict contemporary history, it was thought preferable to choose subjects from the history of French monarchy since the Merovingians until the 17th century, with the equestrian portrait of Henri IV as the main feature. To this effect, pictures were commissioned in 1817-1818 from numerous artists, but the whole set of canvases was not finished until 1826, some of the subjects having been refused and several artists having had to be replaced. Most of these paintings were exhibited at the Salons (1819, 1822, 1824).

The Diana series was entrusted to Merry-Joseph Blondel (1781-1853), a pupil of Regnault who, after having painted some cameos in 1817 to embellish the wall frames in the drawing-room at the end of the gallery, was put in charge in 1820 of all the painting for this room. In 1822, when operations started on the arched ceiling of the gallery,

153. Diana Gallery.

he asked for the assistance of his colleague Alexandre Abel de Pujol (1787-1861). The two artists shared the work, each executing four alternate sections and they finished in 1825. In 1826 Blondel had still to paint the great grisaille picture in the vestibule. During this period of 1817 to 1826, the other parts of the decoration, left unfinished since 1814, were completed and some of the emblems had to be changed after the fall of Napoléon and the return of the Bourbon kings. The carved frieze on the cornice received the royal emblems (Mouret, 1817), the central bay was embellished with a fine carved and gilded wood design, both on the east side, round the frame of Henri IV's portrait (Mou-

154.
Hippolyte Lecomte,
Charlemagne crossing the Alps, 1826.

ret and David d'Angers, 1817), and on the opposite side round the window (David d'Angers, 1817, Guillon, 1818 and Plantar, 1819-1820). In the end room the painted decoration, as in the Empire days, was entrusted to Redouté and Plantar was responsible for the frieze; (he also carved the frieze in the vestibule). In 1822, five inscriptions were placed on the doors of the vestibule and of the opposite room, one indicating LVDOVICVS XVIII INSTAVRAVIT ANNO M DCCC XXII and the four others marked LVDOVICVS XVIII ANNO REGNI XXVIII (of the twenty-eighth year of the reign of Louis XVIII, nominal king since 1795, the presumed date of the death of Louis XVII, his nephew). The wall clock was not delivered by Lepaute until 1827 (though the gilt bronze framework had been chased in 1817 by the chaser Forestier).

Unfortunately this decoration has not been preserved intact, Napoléon III having decided in 1858 to transform the gallery into a library. He placed there the books which Napoléon I had kept in the upper Saint Saturnin Chapel and which he himself, when Prince-Président, had transferred in 1852-1853 above the François I Gallery, where the former 16th-century library had been. The need to find room there for residential apartments had been the reason for putting the Diana Gallery to another use. Sixteen huge oak bookcases were set up, involving the removal of sixteen large historical canvases which were dispersed to various museums in 1875. Only the equestrian portrait of Henri IV by Mauzaisse (1824) and the small-sized pictures still remain: H. Lecomte, *Charlemagne crossing the Alps*, 1826 (fig. 154); F. Richard, *Tanneguy du Châtel saving the Dauphin*, 1819; C.M. Bouton, *Saint Louis at his Mother's Tomb*, 1818; Mme Haudebourt-Lescot, *Diane de Poitiers imploring François I to pardon her Father*, 1819; J.A. Laurent, *Clotilde exorting Clovis to embrace Catholicism before leaving for the Battle of Tolbiac*, 1818; P. Révoil, *The King of Navarre and the Mother of Henri IV*, 1819; F.M. Granet, *Saint Louis ransoming French Prisoners at Damiette*, 1819; J.A. Régnier, *Joan of Arc dedicating herself to the Salvation of France*, 1819. Despite this unfortunate transformation, the Diana Gallery remains one of the most significant ensembles in French art at the time of the Restoration.

Description of the decoration: from the vestibule of the Gallery, the first bays of the vault can be seen.
• First bay by Abel de Pujol: *The Genius of Death, the Genius vanquishing Death.*
Æsculapius in Answer to Diana's Supplication restores Hippolytus to Life (1825).

• Second bay by Blondel: *The Genius of Medicine, the Genius of Pain.*
Latona, fleeing from the Persecutions of Juno, carries off her Children Apollo and Diana (1825).

• Third bay by Abel de Pujol: *The Genius of Impiety, The Genius of Revenge, Diana punishes Oeneus, King of Calydon, who wanted to overthrow the Cult of Diana, by sending an enormous wild Boar to lay Waste to his Realms.*

Above the vestibule door: painting by Blondel of *Diana with her Nymphs*, 1826.

Furniture: from the vestibule of the Gallery, several pieces of furniture and ornaments can be seen: terrestrial globe on a mahogany stand (fig. 155) executed for Napoléon in 1810 by the geographers Jean-Baptiste Poirson and Edme Mentelle and by the mechanician J.L. Merklein (placed in the Tuileries from 1811 to 1829, entered Fontainebleau in 1861); two Cordelier vases with a goat's head in gilt bronze, Manufacture de Porcelaine de Sèvres, Consulate period (entered in 1804).

155.
Terrestrial globe
by the geographers Poirson and Mentelle,
and the mechanician Merklein.

The White Drawing-room
or the Queen's Small Drawing-room

The Queen's cabinet called the Tancred and Clorinda Cabinet. Divided for the Queen's staff around 1730. 1835, Queen's small drawing-room. 1853, Room for the Empress's Ladies-in-Waiting.

Decoration: created in 1835, re-using certain elements of former decorations: Louis-XV woodwork, Louis-XVI chimney garnished with bronze (installed in 1805 in the apartment of Madame Mère, Napoléon's mother).

Furniture: as in Louis-Philippe's day, reconstituted in 1977. Seats in gilded wood upholstered with a brocaded lampas patterned with roses and bees on a green background, made by the Maison Sériziat of Lyon (1811-1813), rewoven by the Maison Prelle in 1980-1981; sofa from the Mars Room at Saint-Cloud, armchairs (stamped Jacob Frères) and chairs brought from the Princes Room at Saint-Cloud, screen made in 1813 by Marcion for Monte Cavallo, footstool, Empire period. Mahogany console table with chimeras in bronzed and gilded wood, Jacob-Desmalter, 1804. Flower stand, Thomire, delivered in 1812 (fig. 156). Gilt bronze pedestal table, Louis XVI (bought from Jacob-Desmalter, 1805). Chandelier, 18th century. Wall-lights with children, Thomire, 1810. Sèvres biscuit clock, The Three Graces, after Chaudet, 1810. Louis-XVI fire-dogs. Sèvres vases, with a gold and platinum pattern on a blue ground, one Medici pair, another one, "etrusque Turpin" form, Louis-Philippe period.

156.
Jardinière by Thomire.

The Queen's Gamesroom
or the Empress's Large Drawing-room

In the 17th and 18th centuries, the Queen's "Grand cabinet", called the Queen's Gamesroom at the end of the *Ancien Régime*. 1804, the Empress's second drawing-room. 1814, the Queen's Gamesroom. 1853, the Empress's drawing-room.

Decoration: walls painted in arabesque style by Michel-Hubert Bourgois and Jacques-Louis-François Touzé from drawings by the architect Pierre Rousseau; ceiling representing *Minerva crowning the Muses* by Jean-Simon Berthélemy; overdoors including *Sacrifices to Mercury* painted in trompe-l'oeil by Sauvage and, below, motifs carved in plaster (female sphinxes and Æsculapius' staff) by Philippe-Laurent Roland, 1786.

Furniture: the furniture existing here at the time of Louis XVI (fig. 157) and that of Napoléon's period (fig. 158) are displayed alternately.
• Furnishing as in Louis XVI's reign: though incomplete, it enables one to evoke the state of the room when the mural decoration was created. The curtains and seats are in a white satin material with a hand-painted design, executed by the Maison Tassinari and Chatel between 1967 and 1981 from an old model taken from the screen. Furniture known by Queen Marie-Antoinette: seats made in 1786 by Sené and Vallois under the direction of Hauré (six folding stools from the Queen's Gamesroom at Compiègne on the same model as those in the Gamesroom at Fontainebleau; two *voyeuse* chairs (for spectators) bought in 1981; folding screen still covered with its original material, gift of Madame François Vernes, 1966; fire-screen purchased in 1951. Two chests of drawers made in 1786 from another piece of furniture due to Stöckel, by the cabinet-maker Beneman, under the direction of Hauré (fig. 159). Other furniture and ornaments: carpet, Savonnerie, Louis-XV period; porcelain vases which could serve as candelabra, Transition period, *circa* 1770; candelabra, "Study" clock, movement by Julien le Roy, fire-dogs with ewers, Louis-XVI period.

157.
The Queen's
gamesroom.

158.
The same room
arranged as the
Empress's Large
Drawing-room.

159.
Commode by Beneman,
after a piece of furniture by Stöckel.

• Furnishing as in the First Empire (reconstituted in 1986): curtains alternately in green and white taffeta. Seats upholstered in green velvet with gold braiding: armchairs, Jacob Frères, Consulate period; footstools, Jacob-Desmalter, 1805; cross-legged stools, three by Jacob Frères, twelve by Jacob-Desmalter; cross-legged folding stools, Jacob-Desmalter, 1806; chairs, Jacob Frères, Consulate period; folding screen, Boulard et Rode, 1806. Carpet with green background, rewoven in 1984-1986 from the original model. Console tables, Jacob-Desmalter, 1804 and 1805. Pedestal table in Sèvres porcelain, known as the Seasons table, painted by Georget from drawings by the architect Brongniart, 1806-1807. Chandeliers in English crystal (war prize, 1805). Two candelabra with a male and female bacchant, early 19th century (purchased from Baudouin, 1804). Four candelabra with winged figures, Consulate period. Candlesticks, Galle, Empire period. Sapho clock, Lepaute, 1804. Eight Sèvres porcelain vases, early 19th century, two "forme Brongniart" with a jasper ground, the others with a blue ground: two "forme bandeau", two with eagle-head handles and two with satyr-head handles. Two ivory vases mounted in gilt bronze, Louis-XVI period. Fire-dogs with fender, adorned with female sphinxes, Consulate period.

The Empress's Bedchamber (Fig. 160)

This was perhaps the Queen's bedchamber from the end of the 16th century, later to become that of all the sovereigns.

Decoration: the central portion of the ceiling, with the monogram of Anne d'Autriche, 1644, by the Paris joiner Guillaume Noyers. Ceiling of the alcove bearing the monogram of Marie Leszczynska, purple breccia marble fireplace (by Trouard) with a carved pier glass, window frames and elements of low wainscotting, 1746-1747. Doors in arabesque style, overdoors in trompe-l'oeil painted by Sauvage, 1787 (antique scenes illustrating *Sleep* and *Dressing*).

Furniture: as in the First Empire (reconstituted in 1986). The material used in this room was woven in Lyon at the end of the *Ancien Régime* by the manufacturer Gaudin, continued by Savournin and purchased by the Garde-meuble royal in 1790. It is a brocaded chenille silk completed by the Widow Baudouin of Paris with embroidery for the seats and the bed. All these silks were used in 1805 in this bedroom. They were rewoven and re-embroidered from the former hangings between 1968 and 1986 (Prelle, Tassinari et Chatel in Lyon); Brocard in Paris). The reconstitution is not yet finished. Only the wall hangings, part of the window curtains, the bed, some of the seats and the screens have been completed. Marie-Antoinette's bed was specially made for this room by Sené et Laurent, under the direction of Hauré in 1787, and was re-used in 1805. Balustrade, Jacob-Desmalter, 1804, for the throne at the Tuileries Palace, remade in 1805. Settee called "*paumier*", Jacob-Desmalter, 1805. Sphinx armchairs, attributed to Jacob Frères, Consulate period (fig. 161). Folding screen and fire-screen, console tables, Jacob-Desmalter, 1806. Chests of drawers

161.
State armchair
attributed to Jacob Frères,
c. 1800 (upholstered in 1986
in silk copied from the original).

by Beneman (see Gamesroom) placed in this bedroom in 1806. Chandelier, Ravrio, 1805. Candelabra, Galle, 1807. Clock with Zephyr and Flora, Lepaute, 1804. Fire-dogs, end of 18th century. Three pairs of Sèvres vases, early 19th century, with a flower and fruit pattern, four "forme etrusque" on a brown ground, two in Medici shape on a blue ground.

160. The Empress's bedchamber.

The Queen's Boudoir (fig. 162)

In the 17th century, the Emperors Chamber or the Queen's cabinet. 1786, the Queen's boudoir. 1804, the Empress's boudoir. 1814, the Queen's boudoir. 1853, the Empress's dressing room.

Decoration: panelling painted by Bourgois and Touzé from drawings by the architect Rousseau (fig. 163), ceiling representing Dawn by Berthélemy, overdoors with high-reliefs in plaster depicting eight of the nine Muses (Terpsichore is missing) by Roland, chimney bronzes and hasps by Pitoin, 1786; mahogany parquet floor, Molitor, 1787.

Furniture: as in Louis XVI's day (incomplete). Cylinder desk (fig. 164) and work-table (fig. 165) in steel, gilt bronze, mother of pearl, made by Riesener in 1786 (both pieces, sold at the Revolution, came back to their original place in 1961). Footstool in gilded and silvered wood, Georges Jacob, 1786 (bought back at a public sale in 1979). Two copies of the only remaining armchair, now held at the Gulbenkian Museum in Lisbon, executed by the Espiritu Santo Foundation in Lisbon, 1977. These seats have been upholstered with an embroidered material, according to the descriptions given in the records.

Passage

On the ceiling, a painting, *Cupids scattering Flowers and Doves,* France, 17th century.

162.
The Queen's boudoir.

163.
The Queen's boudoir,
painted wood panelling.

164.
Rolltop desk belonging to
Queen Marie-Antoinette,
by Riesener, 1786.

165.
Queen Marie-Antoinette's
worktable,
by Riesener, 1786.

Throne Room (fig. 166)

The King's Bedchamber (since the days of Henri III?). 1804, the Emperor's Drawing-room. 1808, Throne Room.

Decoration: the major part of the ceiling, a portion of the low wainscotting, the doors with pediments and bas-reliefs on martial themes, mid-17th century (fig. 167). The medallions above the doors draw their inspiration from tokens of the reign of Louis XIII, one commemorating the struggle against heresy (Hercules crushing the Hydra with his Club, minted in 1636), another one recalling the Capture of Turin and Arras in 1640 (token minted in 1641). Most of the woodwork, 1752-1754 is due to Verberckt and Magnonais. Chimney, 1752. Portrait of Louis XIII, School of Philippe de Cham-

paigne (placed in 1834). The emblems in the room consist of the coats-of-arms of France and of Navarre (ceiling), the emblem of Louis XIII, Hercules' club with the motto: *Erit haec quoque cognita monstris* – the monsters themselves will recognise it (on the wall panelling), Louis XV's monogram (on the ceiling of the former alcove in which stood the King's bed).

Furniture: as it was in the First Empire. Throne composed of a canopy, two ensigns, a dais, an armchair, all made by Jacob-Desmalter in 1804 from designs by the architects Percier and Fontaine, for the Château de Saint-Cloud; they entered Fontainebleau in 1808, except for the armchair which was part of the Tuileries throne. Giltwood stools, Hauré, Sené and Vallois for Marie-Antoinette's Gamesroom at Compiègne,

166.
Throne Room.

167.
Throne Room,
door on the left of the chimney;
overdoor, *Allegory of the Taking of Turin and Arras in 1640*.

168.
Giltwood folding stool
by Sené and Vallois,
1786-1787.

167

168

210. Jean-Baptiste Oudry, *Stag at Bay among the Franchard Rocks, Forest of Fontainebleau*, 1738.

in a white satin damask with gold brocade and silks of the Restoration period made by Grand (entered this room in 1856). Mahogany commode adorned with two unglazed Wedgwood medallions representing the Herculanum dancing girls, porphyra top, stamped Avril (seized from the Comte de Clermont d'Amboise during the Revolution and brought to Fontainebleau in 1857) (fig. 212). Washbasin decorated with swans from a design by Percier and Fontaine, Consulate period (brought from Saint-Cloud to Fontainebleau in 1837). Small worktable "en chiffonnière", Jacob Frères, from a design by these architects, Consulate period (same provenance). Candelabra, bought from Galle, 1807. Clock, Venus putting Love to Sleep, bought from Lepaute, 1804. Fire-dogs, late 18th century, bought from Feuchère, 1805.

This room contains a very fine carpet with the arms of France, made at the Savonnerie factory, Louis-XV period (entered in 1835).

211. Jean-Baptiste Oudry,
Self-portrait, detail of the previous painting.

212. Commode with Wedgwood medallions by Avril, Louis-XVI period.

214. François Gérard, *Napoléon in Coronation Attire*.

Musée
Napoléon Ier

The decision to create a museum devoted to Napoléon at the Château de Fontainebleau was taken in 1979, when the Prince Napoléon, his wife Princesse Napoléon and his sister the Comtesse de Witt arranged to make a gift and an assignment to the French state of part of the imperial family's collection, a prestigious assemblage of historical souvenirs of the First and Second Empire, containing in particular pictures, sculptures, furniture, weapons, decorations, silver and gold ware, and costumes.

Since 1968 the Prince had deposited a good number of these works in the Museums of Bois-Préau and Compiègne. Rather than regrouping them together in a single place, it seemed preferable to distribute them among the two Napoleonic museums already existing and the Musée du Château de Fontainebleau, the vocation of which was defined in relation to them. While Malmaison remained the museum of the Consulate period, of Joséphine and her children, Bois-Préau the museum of St. Helena, the return of Napoléon's ashes and the Napoleonic legend and Compiègne the museum of the Second Empire, Fontainebleau was to become the museum of the Emperor Napoléon I and of his brothers as European kings between 1804 and 1815. Accordingly, Fontainebleau received only a part of the Prince's collections, but in exchange, obtained many works related to the First Empire kept mainly at Malmaison, Bois-Préau, Versailles and the Musée des Arts décoratifs.

The new museum is situated in the Louis XV wing of the Château. Built between 1738 and 1774, it housed from 1803 to 1808 the Ecole spéciale militaire (transferred in 1808 to Saint-Cyr) and was then restored by Napo-

léon. The interior decoration dates for the most part to this period of work (1808-1810). The wing was restored again between 1982 and 1986.

The Musée was inaugurated on 10 June 1986 in the presence of M. Philippe de Villiers, Secrétaire d'Etat à la Culture, and of the Prince and Princesse Napoléon.

Corridor
on the first floor (fig. 213)

With its pictures and busts this is a family gallery.

Paintings: *Marie-Louise* by Madame Benoist, *Murat, Maréchal de l'Empire*, after Gérard. *Cardinal Fesch*, anonymous. *Marie-Julie,*

213.
Musée Napoléon Ier, corridor on the first floor.

Queen of Spain and her two Daughters Zénaïde and Charlotte by Gérard, *Catherine of Würtemberg, Queen of Westphalia*, attributed to Kinson. *Élisa, Grand Duchess of Tuscany and her daughter Napoléon-Élisa*, by Benvenuti. *Justice, Virtue and Wisdom around the Cradle of the Roi de Rome* by A. Rémy.

Sculptures: busts mostly created in the studios of Carrare, under the direction of Bartolini: *Napoléon* after Chaudet. *Marie-Louise* by Triscornia, after Bosio. *Joséphine* after Chaudet. *Pauline* after Canova. *Élisa* after Bartolini. *Félix Baciocchi* after Bartolini. *Lucien* after Marin. *Madame Mère* after Dupaty. *Jérôme* after Bosio. *Catherine of Würtenberg* after Bosio. *Pauline* after Bosio. *Caroline* after Canova. *Hortense de Beauharnais* after Bosio. *Louis* after Cartellier. *Napoléon* by Janssens.

Furniture: benches in gilded wood, Jacob-Desmalter, 1809, covered in green silk velvet. Faience candelabra in imitation of porphyry (Fabry et Utzschneider factory at Sarreguemines, Empire period). Lagrenée porcelain vase with a blue ground, decorated with flowers and fruit (Sèvres Factory, Consulate period).

Room I: Napoléon, Emperor and King

This room is devoted to the two dignities to which Napoléon rose: that of Emperor of the French and that of King of Italy.

The Empire, which followed the Life-Consulate in a virtually logical succession, was adopted by the senatus-consult on 18 May 1804, then ratified by plebiscite and consecrated by the dual coronation and anointing ceremony on 2 December of the same year at Notre-Dame. Soon afterwards, changes in the forms of power in France led to the Republic of Italy becoming a Kingdom. Napoléon who had been President since January 1802 became King of Italy on 24

March 1805 and was crowned in Milan on the following 26 May.

Paintings: *Napoléon in Coronation Attire* by Gérard (1805) (fig. 214). This picture shows in perfect detail the fine costume designed by Isabey and made by the tailor Chevallier, the embroiderer Picot, the furrier Toullet, ..., as well as the imperial ensigns executed by the goldsmith Biennais: crown of laurels, great collar of the Légion d'Honneur, sceptre, orb, hand of Justice. The Emperor is also wearing an emerald ring, mounted by the jeweller Marguerite, and his First Consul sword. The pendant to this painting is *Joséphine in Coronation Attire* (fig. 215), also by Gérard (1807-1808). The Empress's great cape was made at the fashion house of Leroy et Rimbaud and her crown was created by Marguerite.

Sculptures: two plaster busts: *Napoléon* by Chaudet; *Pope Pius VII* by Deseine.

Large showcase: souvenirs of the coronation ceremony are exhibited here, together with what remains of the imperial ensigns, part of the ceremonial costumes of the Emperor, arms, decorations relating to the orders of merit which he instituted. *Souvenirs of the Coronation*: the "Coronation Book" (drawings by Isabey, Percier and Fontaine with their corresponding engravings) recalling the highlights of the ceremony and the costumes of all the participants. Two embroidered cloths served to carry the offerings (Mlles Lolive, de Beuvry et Cie, lingerie-makers). *Imperial ensigns*: the "Coronation" sword made in 1801 by the goldsmith Odiot, the jeweller Nitot and the arms factory at Versailles, had been garnished at the request of the First Consul himself with very valuable diamonds, among which the famous Régent, which he had cleared in payment of debts incurred by the Directoire. It survived in 1815 (when all the rest of the Empire regalia was destroyed) only because it was then no longer part of the imperial jewels. In 1812 Napoléon had had it replaced by a ceremonial sword and its mount, deprived of the diamonds, had been given to the jeweller Nitot to be deducted from his latest invoice.

215. François Gérard, *Joséphine in Coronation Attire.*

Only a modest fragment remains of the famous crown of laurels, one of the gold leaves mounted on a snuffbox which belonged to Isabey. He had unintentionally broken it off when he was trying the crown on the Emperor in 1805, before the coronation in Italy. Napoléon told him to keep it "as a souvenir of his clumsiness", as Isabey himself tells us on the back of the snuffbox. Costumes: all that is left of the ceremonial attire called "grand habillement" is the embroidered tunic, the belt and the model for the shoes. On the other hand, the "petit habillement" Napoléon wore on his way to and from Notre-Dame has been kept (coat, tailcoat, belt) as well as two other tailcoats in purple velvet, two in purple poult-de-soie for the summer and another short coat (fig. 216) which completed the ceremonial robes, as the "small coronation costume" had become the Emperor's official outfit for important ceremonies. The accessories always worn with these clothes included stockings, slippers, gloves, breeches, waistcoats, crossbelts or sword-belts to match. Napoléon also possessed a tailcoat in green velvet which he wore as King of Italy. (Most of these clothes are presented alternately). *Other official arms*: a sword by Biennais, 1806 and a silver sword which Napoléon may have worn at his coronation in Milan. *Decorations*: the Ordre de la Légion d'Honneur, instituted in

216.
Coat made for
Napoléon's second marriage.

1802, did not receive its insignia until 1804. The great collar is the one Napoléon gave to his brother Jérôme. This type of collar seems to have prevailed as early as 1806. The Ordre de la Couronne de Fer, founded in 1805, was the equivalent of the Légion d'Honneur for the kingdom of Italy. It took its name from the antique crown of the Lombard kings, preserved at Monza. The device was "God gave it to me, let he who touches it beware". Finally in 1811 Napoléon created the Ordre Imperial de la Réunion, in favour of the countries united to France, especially Holland, to replace the Ordre de l'Union of his brother Louis. In fact, he intended it for the whole Empire to relieve the demand on the Légion d'Honneur.

Furniture: white and gold folding seats, Marcion, 1806. Clock, Astronomy, Bailly, 1814. Candelabra, early 19th century. Firedogs with female sphinxes, end of 18th century. Round lantern, Louis XVI period.

Room II:
Splendour
of the imperial table

Napoléon considered that ceremonial was an indispensable manifestation of his sovereign power. He had it codified in a book entitled *Etiquette du palais impérial*. It contained a special section on meals divided into three types depending on circumstances: the "grand couvert", the "petit couvert" and meals served in the private apartments. For a *grand couvert* dinner, as in the times of the monarchy, the Emperor needed ceremonial silver. This was acquired in 1804 when the City of Paris offered him a huge service in silver gilt ("Grand Vermeil") made by the goldsmith Henry Auguste, composed of over one thousand pieces. Today only twenty-four of them remain. The imperial table also possessed everyday silver-gilt ware, a large amount of silver as well as porcelain dinner services made for the most part at the Sèvres factory. The most important of all was the Emperor's "service particulier", executed

from 1808 to 1810, part of which Napoléon took with him to St. Helena.

Painting: Alexandre Dufay, known as Casanova (1770-1844), *Banquet at the Wedding of Napoléon and Marie-Louise at the Theatre in the Tuileries, on 2 April 1810* (fig. 217). Here we see the table laid for the *grand couvert*, with several pieces of the *Grand Vermeil* service.

End showcase: the most important pieces from the *Grand Vermeil* service. The two ships are an allusion to the arms of the City of Paris. They are borne by two seated figures of the Seine and the Marne rivers. That of the Emperor (fig. 218) on the right is adorned with the figures of Justice, Truth (poop) and Fame (prow). The one on the left belonged to the Empress and bears the Three Graces (poop) and Welfare (prow). In the centre of the showcase is an olio pot surmounted by a figure of History and two salt-cellars with locks, called "cadenas", where spices were kept.

Large showcase on the left: more of the *Grand Vermeil* service: two tureens with a figure of the Ville de Paris on the lid, a ewer and bowl, three bottle-cooling buckets. *Porcelain*: the Emperor's "service particulier" (fig. 219); nineteen of the seventy-two dessert plates, decorated with subjects "pleasing" to the Emperor (there are eleven views of Egypt and Syria, three of Paris and the outskirts, five of Europe).

Large showcase on the right: more of the *Grand Vermeil*: two tureens adorned with an allegory of the Arts, a bottle-cooling bucket, four glass-cooling basins. *"Ordinaire" silver-gilt ware*: two mustard pots, a coffee-pot, two table knives, by Biennais. *Silverware*: sauceboat and chocolate pot by Genu, two dishes by Genu and Biennais, two plates and a teapot by Biennais. *Porcelain*: soup plate, two fruit bowls and two butter dishes from the Emperor's "service particulier"; three plates from a service with a "fond nankin à figures" decoration, sent to Fontainebleau in 1804 for the arrival of Pope Pius VII; plate representing Bramante

217. Alexandre Dufay, called Casanova, *Banquet at the Wedding of Napoléon and Marie-Louise, 2 April 1810.*

218.
The Emperor's
vermeil nef by
Henry Auguste,
1804.

219.
Cascade in
Wilhelmshöhe Park,
plate from the Emperor's
service particulier in Sèvres porcelain,
subject painted by Lebel in 1808.

Room III: Presents received by the Emperor (fig. 220)

During his reign, Napoléon received many diplomatic gifts, either during visits abroad or through his ambassadors and envoys. Among these there was the table centrepiece offered in 1808 by King Charles IV of Spain when they met in Bayonne. It was a very big tray bearing various monuments in alabaster and semi-precious stones, garnished with cameos and gilt bronze, all made around 1790 in the royal workshops in Madrid (Buen Retiro) under the direction of the Italian G.B. Ferroni. This "surtout", now incomplete, suffered during the First Empire, for the Grand Marshal of the Imperial Household, the Duc de Frioul, thought it was poor in taste and mediocre in quality. The pieces were then either dispersed among imperial palaces, or made into clocks or candelabra, or else broken up. Thirty-one of them have been brought together here (others are found in the private apartments at Fontainebleau – see above p.139 and 140, – at the Grand Trianon, at Versailles, in the Mobilier National and in the Louvre). They include two fountains, a temple-shaped monument, four in the form of an altar, eighteen others changed into candelabra between 1811 and 1813 in Paris by the mosaicist Belloni, two bottle-cooling buckets and four glass-cooling basins.

Besides the diplomatic presents, gifts were exchanged between members of the family. Sometimes they were "sales" in disguise, the "donor" expecting some gratification in return. This was the case with the so-called Venice table, made with polychrome glass mosaic by a Venetian glassmaker called Barbaria. It is a very skilful piece of craftsmanship, consisting of an upper surface in pearl mosaic, a second tray in imitation cameos and precious stones with, in the centre, the head of the Emperor, on the left the imperial eagle, on the right the Italian iron crown, and finally a third tray which served as a writing desk. It was offered to the Emperor in 1811 and he bought it for twenty thousand francs in 1812.

(Italian iconographic service executed at Sèvres in 1813-1814 for the Palace of Rome).

Small showcases: *porcelain*: forty-seven plates from the "Vues diverses" service which started to be made in 1812 at Sèvres and which were delivered to King Louis XVIII to add to part of the personal service Napoléon left behind in Paris. They represent landscapes of Italy (eleven), Spain (thirteen), France (nine), Germany (eight), Great Britain (three), Holland (two), Syria (one).

Furniture: mahogany chairs, end of 18th or early 19th century, which had belonged to General Moreau at the Château de Grosbois. Dining-table, Schiler, Louis-XVI period. Two pier tables, Jacob-Desmalter, 1810. Low bookcase, early 19th century, which had belonged to Murat at the Château de Villiers. Chandelier, Chaumont, 1806. Pair of candelabra, Thomire-Duterme, 1809, for the Emperor's bedchamber at the Tuileries, originally in patinated and gilt bronze and entirely gilded in 1819. Clock, Bréguet, end of 18th century. Fire-dogs, Thomire-Duterme, 1810. Pair of "bandeau" vases in porcelain with a purple marble ground, and decorated with birds, Sèvres factory, 1805-1806. Wall hanging in blue gourgouran silk, rewoven from a model in the Mobilier National.

220. Musée Napoléon Ier, room III.

Furniture: a sofa, two settees, four chairs, 1805; the woodwork was due to Jacob-Desmalter and they are covered with Beauvais tapestry. Side-table in yew-root wood, Consulate period, coming from General Moreau, two side-tables in the same wood, Consulate period, attributed like the preceding one to the merchant Lignereux, successor to Daguerre. Pair of mahogany side-tables, Jacob-Desmalter, 1806. Side-table, Biennais, 1804. Chandelier and fire-dogs, Thomire-Duterme, 1810. Wall-lights, Rabiat and Thomire-Duterme, 1810. Wall hanging in a "spanish-tobacco coloured" damask, with a sunflower design, rewoven in Lyon from an ancient textile by Pernon in 1802-1805 for the Ministers Room at Saint-Cloud (and used in this apartment during the First Empire).

Room IV:
Napoléon's military life

When the Emperor left for the battlefield, he was accompanied by large retinues perfectly well organised. He rode in a mail coach on long journeys, followed by horse-drawn service wagons and vehicles belonging to his household. When he was not too far from his troops, he used a barouche and a series of other barouches preceded and followed him to take his retinue. Halts were made at more or less spacious houses en route, but on the battlefield, tents were set up in the centre of the camp of the imperial guard. Outside, these tents were in blue and white striped drill, edged with a red wool fringe, and they were garnished inside with *toile de Jouy* (cretonne print)

171

To enable the visitor to imagine what the Emperor's tent was like, a copy has been made from one kept at the Mobilier national, though reduced in size and shape in order to fit into this room. In front the so-called "cabinet" (study) is evoked; at the end is the bedroom.

Furniture: small folding table and armchair intended for the Emperor, Jacob-Desmalter, probably 1813, both given by Napoléon himself in 1815 to one of his faithful followers, Charles Schulmeister. Stools for the secretary

and the aide de camp on duty, Jacob-Desmalter. Desk lamp with a removeable shade, Thomire, 1812. Iron bed with an ordinary strap webbing base, model imagined by the locksmith Desouches. Napoléon used similar ones (like the beds at the Musée de l'Armée and at Bois-Préau). "Peau-de-tigre carpet woven from an ancient model.

Right-hand showcase: when campaigning, Napoléon also took with him travelling cases called "nécessaires", containing material for drawing, writing and dining; there were also flasks and sanitary utensils. The showcase contains several of these items, most of them made by the goldsmith Biennais: his large nécessaire n° 4 (1809); a small nécessaire called "de porte-manteau" for it was kept in a sort of suitcase carried at the back of the saddle of the Emperor's mameluk, whenever the Emperor himself travelled on horseback (1812 or 1813) (fig. 221); several objects in vermeil belonging to other sets: a tray, a candlestick, two boxes (from a nécessaire stolen at Waterloo), a plate and goblet by the goldsmith Genu (from the "grand néces-

221.
Napoléon's nécessaire by Biennais.

222.
Napoléon's hunting flask by Biennais.

saire"), a toothbrush and goblet; items in silver: two flasks (fig. 222), a travelling coffeepot, a plate, a metal drinking cup (by the goldsmith Morange), another drinking cup; a knife; a camp bidet in vermeil (incomplete).

Left-hand showcase: here one of the famous overcoats (fig. 223) is displayed which the Emperor wore on top of his uniform in bad weather. At the end of his reign, his wardrobe contained six of them. Most were in grey cloth, but others were in green or blue (a grey and a green one are exhibited in turn). Above, one of the black felt hats worn by the Emperor with his uniforms and which his supplier by special appointment, Poupard, called the "French hat". Altogether there was a dozen of them in Napoléon's wardrobe. Two of the Emperor's spurs are also here, and two pistols from the Versailles factory for the carriages of his retinue, a wallet in morocco with the imperial arms (Despilly, paper-merchant in Paris) which came from the Emperor's carriage pillaged at Waterloo.

223.
Napoléon's
grey overcoat.

Room V:
the Emperor's everyday life

Each day Napoléon wore military attire, either a blue uniform with the white lapels and red turn-ups of a colonel of the Foot Grenadiers of the Guard or the green uniform of a colonel of the "Chasseurs à cheval" of the Guard (at the very end of the reign, he also wore that of the Garde nationale). His time table was well planned. In the morning, after washing and dressing and receiving his entourage, he usually worked in his office with the secretaries. Then the *lever* ceremony took place, followed by audiences and lunch, after which he returned to work, either studying files, receiving ministers and administrative officers or presiding over one of the numerous councils.

In the afternoon, once or twice a week, he went hunting or for a walk, visiting current construction works or public institutions. Dinner, usually partaken with the Empress, was followed by a court reception or a theatre performance. After the retiring (*coucher*) ceremony, Napoléon often continued working. Sundays were devoted to official duties: mass, parades, diplomatic or general audiences, though he dined in private with his family.

Painting: *Napoléon in the Uniform of Colonel of the Foot Grenadiers of the Imperial Guard* by Lefèvre.

Sculpture: *Napoléon at his Desk, Compass in Hand, calculating Distances on a Map*, by Moutoni, a group created in 1808-1809.

Right-hand showcase: presentation of the everyday wear of the Emperor; these clothes are all authentic (the uniform of the Grenadiers (fig. 224) is exhibited alternately with that of the Garde nationale): tailcoat, breeches, waistcoat, sword-belt, duty sword ("épée de service") by Biennais, shoe buckles; on the lapel are the crosses of the Légion d'Honneur and of the Couronne de Fer; on the breast, plaque of the Légion and under the coat the grand cordon of the Légion.

Left-hand showcase: items which belonged to Napoléon. Two sporting guns one by Lepage, the other one (later modified) by Armand, Dombret et Fouquet. Hunting belt. Duty sword identical to the preceding one with case and sword-belt, given by Napoléon to the Grand Duke Constantine of Russia, during the Encounter at Erfurt in 1808. Sword by Biennais garnished with coral from Naples (fig. 225). Snuffbox adorned with two antique silver medallions, executed by Biennais and

225.
Sword embellished
with corals
by Biennais.

224.
Uniform of colonel
of the Foot Grenadiers
of the Imperial Guard,
worn by Napoléon.

Montauban in 1809 (Napoléon liked snuff). Binoculars in the form of a lorgnette, which may have been his (he was shortsighted).

Furniture: the Emperor's mechanical writing desk at the Elysée (supplied by Jacob-Desmalter for Murat). Side-tables in gilt wood (Jacob-Desmalter, 1810). Round pedestal table from a model Napoléon was fond of (Jacob-Desmalter, 1806?). Small settee called "paumier", reconstitution of a seat used every day by Napoléon to read his correspondence. Desk-armchair, Jacob-Desmalter, 1805. Armchairs and chairs upholstered with Beauvais tapestry (furniture of the same set is that on display in Room III). Desk-com-mode, Jacob-Desmalter, 1810. Regulator clock in a mahogany case, Lepaute, 1804. Candelabra with bronze winged victories and others with bronze winged figures, early 19th century. Candelabra in the shape of an obelisk, Ravrio, 1812. Chandelier, Chaumont, 1810. Inkstand from the Emperor's large study at the Tuileries Palace, Biennais, 1806. Vermeil desk lamp (one of twelve ordered from Biennais in 1809, 1811 and 1812). Faïence vase in imitation of porphyry, Fabry et Utzschneider factory at Sarreguemines, 1810. Fire-dogs, Galle, 1806. Wall hangings in green gourgouran woven from a model bought in 1808 from Cartier for the Emperor's topographical room at Fontainebleau.

Room VI: Marie-Louise

Napoléon, at the height of his power, considered that his regime would continue to last only on condition that he produced an heir. Joséphine had to agree to a divorce and the Emperor started negociations to obtain the hand of a foreign princess. The choice finally fell on the eldest daughter of the Austrian Emperor Franz I. Marriage by proxy took place in Vienna on 11 March 1810, the civil marriage at St. Cloud on 1 April and the religious marriage was celebrated in the Salon carré at the Louvre on 2 April (Napoléon's first marriage having been annulled for vice of form). The new Empress was eighteen years old. Thrust for political reasons into the arms of the "ogre", she rapidly became attached to her husband and, despite the baleful influence of her lady in waiting, the Duchesse de Montebello, widow of Maréchal Lannes, and the Emperor's frequent absence from court, from 1812 onwards, she docilely tried to play her role as best she could. Lacking in character, she did not succeed in maintaining her position when confronted with the Allies and her father in 1814.

Paintings and watercolour: the great portrait, replica of an original by Gérard, represents her in full state dress. A watercolour by Garneray depicts one of the episodes of her wedding: *The Imperial Family appearing on the Balcony set up in front of the Façade of the Palais des Tuileries overlooking the Garden* (Salon of 1810). In another picture by Menjaud, an intimate scene reveals Marie-Louise's taste for the arts. She is painting a portrait of her husband.

Sculpture: bust of the Empress by Delaistre (1813).

Showcase: souvenirs of Marie-Louise. Coloured drawing representing Marie-Louise departing from Vienna in 1810. Breakfast-set in Sèvres porcelain (1810-1812), known as the "déjeuner des peines et plaisirs de l'Amour", given by Napoléon to Marie-Louise as a New Year present in 1813, which she left to Madame de Montebello in 1814 (fig. 226). The motifs show the torments and joys that love procures to the soul, represented as a butterfly. Watercolour portrait of the Empress by Isabey (unfinished), presented alternately with another portrait in

biscuit china bas-relief. Two silver statuettes of Napoléon and Marie-Louise (fig. 227) ordered by Denon and cast after antique models by Damerat (1813). Snuffbox adorned with portraits of Napoléon, Marie-Louise and the Roi de Rome (their son), after Isabey. Small almanach for 1811 with the Empress's monogram stamped on the binding. Notebook she gave as a souvenir to Doctor Corvisart.

Furniture: painted-wood seats with mouldings heightened in gold, upholstered with Beauvais tapestry, from the Ministry of the King's Household, tapestries 1811-1815, woodwork 1820. Commode for jewels, Jacob-Desmalter, 1810 for the washroom in Marie-Louise's dressing apartment at the Tuileries. Pedestal table, Marcion, 1806. Chandelier, Duverger, 1804. Wall-lights and fire-dogs, Thomire-Duterme, 1810. Clock with a figure of "Study", Lepaute, 1810. Pair of porcelain Medici vases with a blue ground, Sèvres factory, 1804. Wall hanging in white damask with althæa motifs copied from an ancient textile delivered in 1811 by Séguin for Versailles.

227.
Marie-Louise,
silver statuette,
after the Antique,
by Damerat, 1813.

226.
Déjeuner des peines et plaisirs de l'Amour
Sèvres factory,
1810-1812,
subjects painted by Le Guay.

228.
Musée Napoléon Ier,
room VII, general view with the cradle
of the Roi de Rome by Thomire.

Room VII:
the Roi de Rome (fig. 228)

Napoléon-François-Joseph-Charles, Roi de Rome, was born in the Tuileries on 20 March 1811. This birth, which answered the Emperor's hopes, was saluted by one hundred and one gunshots and the acclamation of the Parisians. The child was entrusted to Comtesse de Montesquiou, governess of the Enfants de France (Princes and Princesses of the Imperial Family). His official role increased with the reverse of fortune suffered by the Emperor. The child then appeared at certain ceremonies and his image was widely diffused to revive loyalty to the regime. Very attached to his father, he had to be dragged out of the Palais des Tuileries on 29 March 1814 (on the eve of the capitulation of Paris to the allied armies). His existence as a young Austrian prince was about to start.

Sculpture: the Roi de Rome appears at the age of a few months in a plaster bust due to the Liège artist Ruxthiel. He is a chubby baby with still undefined features.

Furniture: cradle in elm by Thomire-Duterme (1811). It had been placed in the Roi de Rome's bedroom in the Palais des Tuileries. The craftsman had re-used some parts of the state cradle offered by the City of Paris at his birth which was sent back to the Empress in 1814 (kept at the Hofburg in Vienna). The figure of Victory holding the curtains dates from the Restoration when it replaced the former eagle.

• *Furniture from the young king's apartments*: commode from his bedroom in the Tuileries, Jacob-Desmalter, 1811; seats delivered in 1811 by the upholsterer Maigret for the Emperor's bedchamber at Meudon, which became the child's bedroom when he stayed there: like the walls they are covered with a yellow textile brocaded with flowers, interspersed with fritillaries (or imperial crowns), from the Bissardon, Cousin et Cie factory, rewoven in the 20th century. Clock from the first drawing-room of the new apartment for the Enfants de France on the first floor of the Pavillon de Marsan in the Tuileries,

Lepaute, 1812. Baptistery which served at the unction ceremony in the Tuileries and probably at the baptism in Notre-Dame, goldsmith Pierre Paraud, 1811.

• *Other pieces of furniture* : giltwood console, Marcion, 1808. Chandelier, Chaumont, 1806. Wall-lights and fire-dogs, Thomire-Duterme, 1810. Two porcelain vases, with children and tritons, one with a grey background adorned with a landscape, the other on a stone-coloured ground, Sèvres factory, 1800, 1803.

Room VIII:
the Roi de Rome

Painting: his portrait by Gérard dates from the summer of 1812 (fig. 229). The Empress commissioned it to be sent to Napoléon in Russia. The original painting is known to have reached the imperial headquarters on 6 September, on the eve of the battle of the Moskowa, and Napoléon had it placed in front of his tent for the officers and soldiers of the Garde to see.

Showcase: copy of the famous drawing executed by Prud'hon showing the head of the

229.
François Gérard,
The Roi de Rome,
1812.

child asleep. Watercolour by Louis Lafitte, allegory of birth: this was a project for the Senate. The Senate, personified by Minerva, is leaning over the King's cradle; below is the she-wolf succouring Romulus and Remus. Several souvenirs originating from the descendants of Madame Soufflot, "première femme" of the King who, having become "sous-gouvernante" in April 1814, accompanied the Prince to Vienna and stayed with him until October 1815: a sabre, trinkets, a rattle, a small plaque of the Légion d'Honneur, a gun by De Saint Etienne, beltmaker to the Emperor (fig. 230), a dagger made at the royal factory in Naples, a hussard's sword-belt, a cartridge pouch, a method to learn to read, *Le Quadrille des Enfants*, consisting of a book and a box of cards. Other objects which appear to have belonged to the Prince: a collar of the Golden Fleece, a cross of the Légion d'Honneur, a drum, a set of dominoes, a cannon (on a reconstituted mount), a game of patience in ivory, an artillery vehicle, a valuable item made by the goldsmith Douault-Wieland (1814) which was found in the Tuileries in 1815.

Furniture:

• *Furniture from the King's apartments*: commode for the King's bedchamber at Saint-Cloud, formerly the Empress Joséphine's private apartment, Consulate period, attributed to the Jacob brothers.

• *Other pieces of furniture and ornaments*: chandelier, Duverger, 1804. Wall-lights and fire-dogs, Thomire-Duterme, 1810. Clock, Love's Chariot, Bailly, 1806. Bronze gilt vases, late 18th century. On the commode, two plaster fragments intended to serve as models for a porcelain vase which was to be made at the Sèvres factory to illustrate the devolution of the regency to Marie-Louise on 30 March 1813, F. Rude, from a drawing by A.E. Fragonard.

Room VIII bis: the Roi de Rome

This room is devoted to the Roi de Rome's baby linen: most of it was given by the descendants of Madame de Montesquiou. These baby clothes were delivered by the Widow Minette, linen-draper in Paris (for forty thousand francs), Lesueur, lace-seller in Paris (for sixty thousand francs) and Bonnaire, lacemaker in Caen (eighteen thousand eight hundred francs).

Showcase: various items are presented in rotation: robes, vests, bonnets, scarfs, slippers, pillowcases, cradle coverlets, nankeen costume.

Painting: *Napoléon at Lunch, is holding the Roi de Rome in his Arms, in the Presence of Marie-Louise, Madame de Montesquiou, Madame Auchard, the Prince's Nurse and Regnault de Saint-Jean d'Angely*, by Menjaud (Salon of 1812).

Furniture: cradle ordered from Jacob-Desmalter by Madame de Montesquiou in 1810 in preparation for the royal birth and placed in the Prince's apartment at Saint-Cloud in 1811.
Chairs, Jacob-Desmalter, 1806. Console table, Jacob-Desmalter, 1804. Wall-lights, Ravrio, 1805. Clock, "Motherly Sollicitude", Bailly, 1806. Fire-dogs with cornucopia, Ravrio, 1812. Lantern, Empire period.

Central staircase

The walls are decorated with panels of painted velvet, executed in 1811 at the Delaneuville et Cie factory in Paris (managers: Louis-Joseph Leroy and Antoine Vauchelet) to furnish the Roi de Rome's reception room at the Senate. The largest one, the view of the Forum in Rome, replaced during the Restoration the panel commemorating the Prince's birth.

On the ground floor a picture serves as an introduction to the imperial family's rooms. The artist remains unidentified and the work is unfinished. The scene represented concerns an episode in the life of Jérôme, King of Westphalia: his Lifeguards are taking the oath in front the Orangery in Kassel.

Room IX: Madame Mère

The Emperor's mother was a noble figure. Born Maria-Letizia Ramolino, she became a widow at the age of thirty-five. In charge of eight children, she showed in every circumstance unfailing courage and dignity. During the Empire she was made an imperial highness and was generously endowed by her son which enabled her to live a discreet life of ease. Madame had a mansion in Paris (Hôtel de Brienne, now the Ministry of Defence) and the Château de Pont-sur-Seine. She played no part in politics but frequently intervened in family disputes, often taking sides against the Emperor. Nevertheless, after his fall, she was full of sollicitude for Napoléon and tried to soften his captivity. She retired to Rome where she died a very old woman in 1836, unanimously respected.

230.
Gun made for the Roi de Rome by de Saint-Etienne, the Emperor's beltmaker.

Painting: portrait of Madame Mère, after Gérard (fig. 231).

Showcase: pieces from a table service in vermeil, by the goldsmith Odiot, marked 1798-1809, acquired by Madame Mère in 1806: oval dishes, plates, spoons, forks, serving spoons; knives by the cutler Gavet.

Furniture: seats in mahogany (Boulard, 1806) and screen (Marcion, 1810) covered in buff gourgouran. Commode, Consulate period. Console, Jacob-Desmalter, 1805. Pedestal table, Lerpsher, 1809. Wall-lights with swan's necks, Thomire-Duterme, 1812. Clock, Lepaute, 1806. Fire-dogs, Thomire-Duterme, 1810. Pair of "âge anse grecque" vases and a Medici vase in porcelain with a stone ground, Sèvres factory, 1803.

Room X: Joseph

Napoléon's eldest brother Joseph (born in 1768), rose to the highest ranks thanks to the Emperor. During the constitution of the Empire, he was named a French prince, Grand Elector of the Empire and declared the first heir in line of succession after his brother's legitimate or adopted children. At the wish of Napoléon he then played a part in the system of reorganisaton of Europe by accepting the crown of Naples in 1806 and then that of Spain in 1808. Even though he was well accepted in Naples, despite certain difficulties, this was not the case in Spain where the uprising against the invader was widespread, obliging Napoléon to maintain considerable forces there to support him. Joseph lacked the necessary authority to ensure cohesion between the diverse French generals. After the battle of Vitoria (June

231.
François Gérard (after),
Madame Mère.

1813), won by Wellington, he was forced to abandon the country. Napoléon appointed him Lieutenant-General during the campaign in France. It was in this capacity that he organised the Empress's departure from Paris on 29 March 1814 and authorised the capitulation of the capital. Joseph was an honest man, but he was never able to dominate events.

Paintings: in a large portrait Gérard has represented him as King of Spain and of India, in full royal attire. From his marriage to Marie-Julie Clary (1771-1845), a merchant's daughter from Marseille, Joseph had two daughters, Zénaïde and Charlotte. Robert Lefèvre portrayed them in 1805 at the respective age of four and three (fig. 232).

Sculpture: bust of King Joseph, after Delaistre (fig. 233).

Showcase: diverse weapons which belonged to King Joseph: an Eastern sabre which may have been seized from Mourad Bey by General Bonaparte, three swords, two ceremonial swords, a hunting knife, as well as a very large set of pistols made at the arms factory in Versailles. Napoléon had probably offered this case to Joseph on his departure for Spain in 1808. Some decorations recall here that in 1808, as King of Naples, Joseph created the Royal Order of the Two Sicilies and in 1809, when he was King of Spain, the Royal Order of Spain.

Furniture: armchairs and chairs, Jacob-Desmalter, 1805-1806, covered in green gourgouran. Console, Marcion, 1809. Commode, Jacob-Desmalter, 1810. Wall-lights, Rabiat and Thomire-Duterme, 1810. Clock, Nymph on a rock, white marble, Lepaute, early 19th century. Fire-dogs, Thomire-Duterme, 1810.

232.
Robert Lefèvre,
Zénaïde and Charlotte,
Joseph's Daughters,
1805.

233.
François-Nicolas Delaistre (after),
Joseph.

Room XI: Louis

Born in 1778, Napoléon's favourite brother Louis Bonaparte, was of an anxious sickly temperament. His marriage in 1802 to Hortense de Beauharnais, the Premier Consul's stepdaughter, almost immediately proved a failure, further unbalancing his character. Yet the creation of the Empire meant a shower of honours for him. Already general and state councillor, in 1804 he was appointed French prince and high dignitary of the Empire. Then, in 1806, Napoléon had him proclaimed king of Holland. Misunderstanding between the two brothers soon became chronic, Napoléon wanting Louis to be his devoted lieutenant, carrying out all his commands, particularly regarding the blocus with England, while Louis tried to take into account the interests of his subjects to the detriment of those of

France. Difficulties piled up to such a point that Louis ended by abdicating in 1810, which resulted in Napoléon reuniting Holland to the Empire. This was the most serious false note in the harmonious family system built up by Napoléon.

Painting: the figure of this honest king is evoked in a portrait by the English artist C.H. Hodges (1809) (fig. 234).

Drawing and print: *Arrival of King Louis at the Royal Palace in Amsterdam, 20 April 1808.*

Showcase: weapons which had belonged to him: Eastern sabre which he may have worn in Egypt, four swords, two sabres (one executed by Schimelbach & Sons at Solingen), ceremonial sword. Two crowns which deco-

234.
Charles Howard
Hodges,
*Louis,
King of Holland.*

rated one of his carriages. Decorations of the Order of Merit which he founded in 1806 and which was finally called the Royal Order of the Union in November 1807. Napoléon suppressed the Order and replaced it by the Order of the Reunion.

Furniture: seats with swan's necks, Marcion, 1805, upholstered with material like the original figured yellow and white gourgouran. Screen, Marcion, 1810. Console, Jacob-Desmalter, 1806. Commode and secrétaire with Egyptian heads, Baudouin, 1804. Wall-lights, Galle, 1806. Clock, Anacreon, Lepaute, 1806. Fire-dogs, Thomire-Duterme, 1810. Pair of etruscan porcelain vases with a green background, heads of Bacchus and Ariadne, Sèvres factory, 1815. Covered porcelain vase with eagles' heads, tortoiseshell ground with flower motifs, Sèvres factory, 1800.

Room XII: Jérôme

Jérôme, born in 1784, was the youngest member of the Bonaparte family. He entered the Navy during the Consulate and in 1803 he married a young American girl from Baltimore, without permission. Napoléon had the marriage annulled in 1805. Jérôme became a French prince in 1806. He then launched forth on an exceptional career for, despite his young years, the Emperor had him recognised as King of Westphalia at the Treaty of Tilsit after having formed a kingdom made up of the Hesse Electorate, a portion of Hanover and some territories taken from dismantled Prussia. Napoléon arranged his marriage to the daughter of the King of Würtenberg. Thus Jérôme served as an instrument of the Emperor's policy which consisted here in extending French domination

235.
François-Joseph
Kinson,
*Jérôme,
King of Westphalia.*

over the whole of Germany. Despite the artificial character of the new kingdom, the unreliability of the young prince and the influence of ill-chosen followers who took advantage of the situation, Jérôme managed to be accepted by his subjects and remained in power until the autumn of 1813. However, he was under surveillance and Napoléon often called him to order. Though his attitude during the Austrian campaigns in 1809 and those in Russia in 1812 was questionable, he fought with great courage at Waterloo. Jérôme was a likeable person.

Painting: he appears here in a picture executed by his First Painter, the Flemish F.J. Kinson (fig. 235), in a romantic pose, seated in the park of the Castle of Napoleonshöhe (ex Wilhelmshöhe) near Kassel.

Drawing: hilt of a sword belonging to Napoléon who bequeathed it to his brother Jérôme.

Showcase: his features are recognisable in a small biscuit porcelain bust made at the Furstenberg factory after a model by the German sculptor Ruhl. Jérôme loved luxury and spent money recklessly. Several works exhibited here testify to his taste: the breastplate (fig. 236) and helmet which he ordered from Boutrais in 1811, a Paris hatter specialising in military equipments (the ornamentation was partly due to the goldsmiths Biennais and

Robert), the royal sword of Westphalia and another sword, both from the workshops of Biennais, a tea fountain by the same goldsmith. Like all members of the Napoléon family, Jérôme created an order of merit, the Order of the Crown of Westphalia (25 December 1809). A cross of this Order is embellished with pearls (Gibert, goldsmith in Paris). Jérôme also possessed some fine decorations of the orders he had received from his brothers: the Iron Crown, the Royal Order of the Two Sicilies, the Royal Order of Holland. Other souvenirs evoke his career as sovereign: a sabre and a naval dagger; a travelling case offered by Napoléon on 9 October 1806; a plate painted by Spangenberg at Göttingen, representing an episode of the Austrian campaign (1809) in which the King saved one of his lifeguards from drowning. Other souvenirs of Jérôme and Catherine are exhibited alternately with the sovereign's clothes, a court costume elaborately embroidered and a uniform of colonel of the Lifeguards of Westphalia.

Furniture: armchairs in painted wood covered in Beauvais tapestry, 1808. Small console, Marcion, 1805. Side-table, Jacob-Desmalter, 1805. Wall-lights, Thomire-Duterme, 1812. Clock, Euterpe and Erato, Lepaute, 1806. Fire-dogs, Galle, 1806. Pair of "Percier" vases in porcelain with a reddish-brown ground and bas-reliefs by Sauvage, Sèvres factory, 1805-1806.

236.
Jérôme's breastplate
by Boutrais and Biennais,
1811.

237. Musée Napoléon Ier, room XIII, general view.

Room XIII: *Élisa* (fig. 217)

238. François-Joseph Kinson,
Élisa, Grand-Duchess of Tuscany.

Maria-Anna, known as Élisa, was born in 1777 and she married a Corsican army captain, Félix Baciocchi, when she was twenty. During the Consulate she already began to play a role by gathering artists and writers around her. In 1805 Napoléon gave the Baciocchi couple the principalities of Lucca and Piombino, but in reality it was Élisa who held the power in her hands; she was an intelligent woman, anxious to imitate her brother and to give proof of her good sense of political matters. In 1809 she obtained from him the administration of Tuscany with the title of Grand Duchess and a residence in Florence.

Sculptures: Élisa played an important role in the sphere of arts, thanks notably to the presence on her territories of the marble quarries of Carrare. From there came the three statues exhibited in this room, all created by the Florentine sculptor Bartolini: the full-length statue of Élisa and her daughter Napoléon-Élisa, the bust of the little girl and the statue of her baby brother Jérôme Charles (who died in 1811 at the age of nine months).

Paintings and drawing: the oil portrait of Élisa (fig. 238) seems to have been com-

187

missioned by King Jérôme and painted by F.J. Kinson in 1810, whereas that of his daughter was painted by Madame Benoist (Salon of 1810) for Élisa herself. The drawing representing the head of Camille from the *Oath of the Horatii* by David was copied by Élisa, during the Consulate period.

Furniture: in the centre of the room stands a curious piece of furniture, a mechanical desk created by a Florentine cabinetmaker, Giovanni Socci (fig. 239). It appears to date from 1807 and to have been made for the Queen of Etruria, Marie-Louise de Bourbon. After the fall of the Empire, it was given back to Élisa. Other pieces of furniture and objects: two bergère armchairs, eight armchairs with Egyptian heads, four chairs, Jacob-Desmalter, 1805-1806 and a fire-screen, Maigret, 1807, covered with yellow gourgouran. Console, Jacob-Desmalter, 1805. Commode in yew with inlays, Jacob-Desmalter, 1804. Wall-lights, Thomire-Duterme, 1810. Fireguard with female sphinxes, early 19th century. Clock, Virgil and his Muse contemplating the bust of Homer, Ravrio the bronzesmith and Porchez the clockmaker, early 19th century.

Room XIV:
Pauline

Pauline (1780-1825) was a famous beauty. Married first to General Leclerc who died of yellow fever during the Saint Domenico expedition (1802), she married again in 1803, this time Prince Camillo Borghese, head of a long-established Roman family. Pauline took no part in politics. Separated from her husband she led a somewhat frivolous life, spending her time between Paris, Neuilly and various spa towns. In 1814 she manifested her deep loyalty to her brother and went to stay with him on the Island of Elba. Canova the sculptor has immortalised her as the Venus Victorious in the famous Beauty Contest among the Goddesses (Rome, Villa Borghese).

Painting: the portrait (fig. 240) exhibited here is a more modest work of art, painted by Madame Benoist mentioned above.

Showcase: the only other souvenir, two vermeil dish-covers and their hot-plates, by Biennais, bearing the Borghese arms.

239.
Mechanical desk
by the Florentine cabinetmaker Socci.

Furniture: a settee, a bergère. four arm-chairs, four chairs, two footstools and a screen, Jacob-Desmalter, 1810, covered with a green damask similar to the original, rewoven in 1810 in Lyon from the old pattern by Grand Frères. Commode with a "turkish" decoration, Jacob-Desmalter, 1810. Pedestal table, Marcion, 1806. Secrétaire and chiffonnier, Rocheux, 1810. Side-table, Clément, 1804. Wall-lights, Thomire-Duterme, 1810. Medici vase clock with figures, Lepaute, 1806. Fire-dogs with bas-reliefs of Fame, Galle, 1806. Pair of porcelain "fuseau" vases with a blue ground, medallions with antique heads, Sèvres factory, 1804. Another pair with a blue background, also in Sèvres porcelain, 1808-1854.

Room XV: Caroline

Caroline's destiny is inextricably mingled with that of Joachim Murat whom she married at the age of eighteen in 1800. By this time Murat had already proved his valour in Italy and Egypt. Commander of the Garde des Consuls, Governor of Paris, he took part as a cavalry man in all military operations, rendering great service to Napoléon. His rise was brilliant: marshal in 1804, prince and admiral in chief in 1805, Grand Duke of Berg in 1806, King of Naples in 1808. His wife was extremely ambitious and it was she who begged her brother to give her husband the throne of Naples. The Murats were a success in Naples and tried gradually to free

240.
Marie-Wilhelmine Benoist,
Pauline, Princess Borghese.

241. François Gérard, *Caroline with her Children.*

themselves from the authority of the Emperor, ending up by betraying him in 1813-1814 when they aligned themselves with the allies and thereby saved their position. During the Hundred Days, Murat turned his coat once again in favour of Napoléon, but this time he did not succeed. He could no longer hope to reach his goal which was to conquer Italy and make it independent. Napoléon refused his services. After disembarking in

Calabria, he was shot at Il Pizzo on 13 October 1815.

Paintings: the fine portrait of Caroline was painted by Gérard in 1808 (fig. 241). The Queen is surrounded by her four children: from left to right, Louise, the future Comtesse Rasponi, Achille, Prince Royal of Naples, Lucien, and Letizia who became Marchesa Pepoli. Letizia appears alone in Madame

Chaudet's picture. She is holding in her arms the bust of her uncle Napoléon (Salon of 1806).

Sculpture: bust of Caroline in biscuit porcelain (Royal Factory of Naples) (fig. 242). Two patinated gilt bronzes, Joachim and Caroline in triumphal chariots, Naples, 19th century.

Furniture: chesstable, adorned with coral, made in the royal workshops in Naples (could have been given by Caroline to her brother). Mahogany seats, Jacob-Desmalter, 1805-1806, covered with a blue gourgouran, like the original material, with orange and black braiding. Fire-screen, Maigret, 1807. Two consoles, Marcion, 1806. Console, Clément, 1805. Two consoles, Baudouin, 1804. Wall-lights, Thomire-Duterme, 1810. Patinated gilt bronze architectural clock, Lepaute, 1804. Two porcelain "fuseau" vases with a tortoiseshell ground and a gilt decoration, Sèvres factory, 1801. Fire-dogs, Ravrio, 1806.

242.
Royal Manufactory of Naples,
Caroline,
bust in biscuit.

1786-1787 (fig. 168). Folding screen and fire-screen in Louis-XVI style, Boulard, Rode et Chatard, 1805. Console tables in gilded wood with lions' heads, Jacob-Desmalter, 1808 (fig. 169). Candelabra in giltwood, Jacob-Desmalter, and girandoles mounted by Thomire, 1808. Table on which the higher officials of the Empire took the oath, 1813. Chandelier, Chaumont (purchased from M. de Bausset, Préfet du Palais, 1808) (fig. 170). Four candelabra with martial trophies, Thomire, 1808. Candlesticks, Empire period. Wall clock, Lepaute, 1808. Fire-dogs, Louis-XVI period. Carpet with military motifs, Manufacture de la Savonnerie, woven from a model of the carpet in Napoléon's bedroom at the Tuileries, designed by the architect Saint-Ange, 1811-1813.

Passage

Formerly the room of the King's head valet. According to tradition, after the Council had held session, the papers were burnt there.

Mural decoration by Alexis Peyrotte, 1753.

169.
Console table by Jacob-Desmalter, 1808.

170.
Chandelier in gilt bronze and rock crystal, by Chaumont, early 19th-century, bought secondhand in 1808.

Council Room (fig. 171)

Madame's (François I's mother) cabinet from 1528 to 1531. The King's cabinet, becoming later the King's first cabinet or the King's small bedroom. Since 1737, is called the "Grand Cabinet" or the Council room.

Decoration: 1751-1753 (except the hemicycle): on the ceiling there are five canvases by Boucher, *The Sun sets forth on its Course and chases Night away* (fig. 172) and *The Four Seasons*. On the panelling and the doors, virtues and allegories of the seasons and the elements by Carle Van Loo and Jean-Baptiste Pierre, in camaieu, alternately pink (Pierre) and blue (Van Loo): *Valour, Autumn* and beneath *Earth, Winter* and beneath *Fire, Fame, The Secret* (on the Throne Room wall); *Fidelity, Peace, War, Might* (on the chimney wall); *Clemency, Truth, Spring* and beneath *Air, Summer* and beneath *Water, History* (fig. 173) (on the Emperor's bedchamber wall). On the two last doors (one of which has been removed) are *Justice* and *Prudence*. Ornaments of flowers, trophies of the Sciences and the Arts, and overdoors in camaieu by Alexis Peyrotte: *Painting and Sculpture, Hunting, Morning, The Navy, Fishing* (Throne Room wall): *Trade, Abundance, War, Architecture* (chimney wall), *Music, Geometry, Evening, Astronomy, The Sciences* (the Emperor's bedchamber wall). Hemicycle, 1773: *Glory surrounded by Putti* by Lagrenée le Jeune, trophies of the Harvest and Grape-picking and ornaments by François-Gabriel Vernet. Above the doors, two inscriptions DITAT ET ORNAT: he [the King] enhances and adorns [the room] – SPLENDOR AB HOSPITE: the splendour [of the room] is due to him who lives in it [the King]. On the ceiling, monogram of Louis XV.

173.
Carle Van Loo, *History*.

172. François Boucher, *The Sun sets forth on its Course and chases Night away*.

171. The Council Room.

Furniture: as it was in the First Empire. The silks in this room, rewoven between 1966 and 1972, include a crimson damask with crowns and stars, the brocaded borders with an oak-leaf pattern (for the seats) and a palm motif for the curtains) which were ordered in 1804 at the Pernon factory in Lyon for the Emperor's bedchamber at Saint-Cloud. Seats: two armchairs, thirty folding stools by Marcion (1806), two armchairs and six chairs by Jacob-Desmalter (1808). Two console tables in gilded wood, executed in 1774 especially for this room (they were not sold at the Revolution). Council table covered with a green silk velvet cloth. Chandeliers in the Louis-XV style (entered in 1854). Four candelabra with military trophies, Galle, 1807. Wall-lights and a covered desk lamp, Empire period. An arched "milestone" clock in black marble with a figure of Study, Lepaute, 1808 (fig. 174). Firedogs, Louis XVI period. Carpet rewoven in 1981 from the Tournai factory original.

174.
"Milestone"
clock with a figure of
Study, delivered by the
clockmaker Lepaute
in 1808.

Rooms undergoing restoration:

The Emperor's Bedchamber

1786, the King's Powder Room. 1804, the Emperor's Study. 1808, the Emperor's Bedchamber. From 1815 to 1870, the bedchamber of all the sovereigns.

Decoration: carved woodwork by Laplace, chimney by the sculptor Roland, six overdoors by Sauvage representing Cupids making sacrifices and forming processions, 1786. Mural decoration with "rehaussé d'or", painted by Simon-Frédéric Moench, 1811 (fig. 175).

175.
Detail of the "rehaussé d'or" mural decoration in the Emperor's bedchamber: figure of Victory.

The Emperor's small bedroom

1786, the King's study, 1804, the Emperor's bedchamber. 1808, the Emperor's library and study. 1811, the Emperor's small bedroom. 1814, the King's small bedroom. 1832, the King's study. 1853, the Emperor's study.

Decoration: chimney, 1786. Two overdoors by Sauvage: Women putting flowers round a tripod table, 1786. Mural decoration painted by Jean-Baptiste Regnault, *Royal Clemency stopping Justice in her Course*, allegory of the return of the Bourbons to France, 1818 (fig. 176).

The Emperor's private drawing-room, called the Abdication Room

1786, Louis XVI's library. 1804, the Emperor's bathroom. 1808, the Emperor's drawing-room. 1814, the King's study. 1832, the Abdication Room. 1853, the Emperor's private drawing-room.

Decoration: ceiling cornice, end of 18th century. Chimney in Italian griotte marble and gilt bronzework, by the marble carver Hersent and the caster Forestier, 1805.

Room of the Emperor's Aides-de-camp

1786, Louis XVIth's bathroom called "*pièce des cuves*". 1804, Eugène de Beauharnais' antechamber. 1806, room for the Emperor's aides-de-camp. 1814, Room for the King's valets. 1832, study of the King's secretary. 1853, study of the Emperor's secretary.

Decoration: chimney, 1786. Decoration of the walls and doors. 1808 (renovated in 1986).

The Emperor's Antechamber

1786, Louis XVI's "chambre des bains". 1804, Eugène de Beauharnais's bedroom. 1805, topographical room. Since 1808, antechamber.

Decoration: five overdoors placed in 1841: P. Toutain, *Two Muses*; J. Durand, *Sleep*, 1742. French School of the 18th century: three pictures: *Children's Games* (allegories of hunting and fishing). Two large paintings placed in 1859: J.M. Vien, *Hector persuading Paris to take up Arms*, 1783, and N. Brenet, *Roman Ladies offering their Jewels to the Senate*, 1785.

176.
Jean-Baptiste Regnault,
*Royal Clemency
stopping Justice
in its Course,*
1818.

179.
Temple clock,
Madrid,
Buen Retiro factory,
c. 1790,
Thomire and Lepaute, 1810.

Private apartments
Stags Gallery
Queen's Staircase
Hunts Apartment

Private apartments of the Emperor and the Empress

The private apartments are situated on the ground floor in three different buildings: the François I Gallery wing (1528), the Louis XVI wing doubling it (1785-1786) and the wing of the royal apartments looking on to the Diana garden (1565-1570), rearranged in the reign of Louis XV.

From 1541-1545 onwards, the part beneath the Gallery contained the king's Baths Apartment, a suite of six rooms comprising the bathrooms themselves and the rest rooms, in the largest of which, on 4 May 1600, the famous conference on the Catholic and Protestant religions was held, hence the name of Conference Room which it bore in the 17th century. The decoration made for François I disappeared in 1697 when Louis XIV gave the apartment to one of his legitimised daughters, the Dowager Princesse de Conti.

There is no record earlier than the reign of Louis XIV of the occupants of the Charles IX wing beyond. Though Monseigneur (the Dauphin) appears to have lived there, the main residents at this time were Madame de Montespan, her sons the Duc du Maine and the Comte de Toulouse and later, in Louis XV's reign, the Duchesse du Maine and her two sons, the Prince de Dombes and the Comte d'Eu. Between their apartments and that of the Princesse de Conti, beneath the king's bedchamber and closet, was the lodging of the Duc de La Rochefoucauld, Grand-Maître de la Garde-Robe (the king's wardrobe being on the ground floor of the Keep).

When Louis XV decided at the end of 1735 to have some private rooms arranged for him on the ground floor, he took part of La Rochefoucauld's and Conti's apartments for this purpose. The death of the Princesse de Conti in 1739 enabled him to enlarge it still more (while giving the rest of her apartment to the Duc de Chartres, then to the Lauraguais). The intimate character of these rooms was further emphasized by the fact that the King accorded to his successive favourites an apartment next door to his. In 1743 Madame de La Tournelle took the place of Monsieur de La Rochefoucauld, in 1745 Madame de Pompadour succeeded her, then, owing to work undertaken in the Queen's apartment in 1746, the King installed the Marquise de Pompadour on the opposite side near the chapel, where she remained until her death in 1764. After several fleeting occupants – in 1765 the Maréchal d'Estrées and his wife, in 1766 the widowed Dauphine, in 1767 the Duc de Penthièvre, – the King's last favourite, Madame du Barry, lived there from 1769 to 1774.

On the other hand, in 1750, the elder princesses, Adélaïde and Henriette moved out of the Stove Pavilion when Louis XV decided to have it pulled down and went to live near their father in apartments which had been occupied by Madame de La Tournelle and Madame de Pompadour. After the death of Madame Henriette, Madame Adélaïde was joined in 1752 by Madame Victoire, then in 1754 by her younger sisters Sophie and Louise who took over the former Maine apartment. They stayed there until the Journey in 1778 [1], in the reign of

1. Once a year the King with the court took up residence at Fontainebleau.

Louis XVI (except for Madame Louise who had become a Carmelite nun at Saint-Denis in 1770). As the new king had no mistresses, the Du Barry apartment was occupied by the Comtesse de Maurepas, then in 1783 by the Princesse de Lamballe. Louis XVI used his grandfather's private rooms for himself and in 1783 his aunts' apartment became that of the royal children: Madame Royale, the Dauphin and the Duc de Normandie. The new wing, erected in 1785-1786 alongside the François I Gallery, provided room for the King's new private apartment and for Madame Élisabeth, the King's sister (near the chapel).

After the turmoil of the Revolution a new court was installed in the Château in 1804. During the Pope's visit, Napoléon lodged his brother Prince Joseph, Cardinal Caprara, Grand Marshall Duroc and Cardinal Fesch all here on the ground floor. Soon afterwards, in 1805, the furniture was removed and, pending an imperial decision on how the rooms were to be allocated, a few were allotted to Joséphine's lady-in-waiting, the Comtesse de La Rochefoucauld, and to Bacler d'Albe, in charge of the Emperor's topographical office. In 1808 the apartment which had belonged to the royal children became the Empress's private apartment and Louis XVI private rooms were turned into offices for the Emperor. The Emperor's private apartment was arranged in 1810 in the one formerly occupied by Madame Élisabeth.

These private apartments which had been furnished for Napoléon and Joséphine passed during the Restoration to the Duc and Duchesse d'Angoulême (Dauphin and Dauphine in 1824), except for the Emperor's library which still belonged to the King's apartment. In Louis-Philippe's reign, the apartment of the Duc d'Angoulême was given to Madame Adélaïde and the King's daughters, Princesse Marie and Princesse Clémentine, and later Princesse Clémentine and her husband, Duke August of Saxe-Coburg, occupied that of the Duchesse d'Angoulême. Apart from the library, the Emperor's former offices now formed a separate apartment called "*du col du cygne*" (Swan's Neck), which took its name from the fountain in Louis XVI's former Buffet Room.

During the Second Republic and at the time of Napoléon III, among the people who lodged here in the part which had been occupied by Napoléon were: Princesse Mathilde (1850), Prince Napoléon (1853), the Comte and Comtesse Walewski (1857, 1858, 1859), the Comte and Comtesse de Pourtalès (1862, 1864) and the Marquis and Marquise de Roccagiovine, the Emperor's cousins (1864); in the part formerly occupied by Joséphine and Marie-Louise: the British ambassador Lord Cowley (1853, 1857), the Prince and Princesse Joachim Murat (1857), the Comtesse de Montijo, the Empress's mother (1858), the Prince and Princesse de Metternich (1860); in the Emperor's former offices: the Czartoryski (1860, 1861), the Primoli (1864) and the Comte de Goltz (1864).

The Emperor's antechamber

Madame de Pompadour's first and then second antechamber. First antechamber of Madame Élisabeth (1791).

Furniture: antechamber seats in painted wood made for this room in 1810 (replaced in 1972).

The Emperor's first drawing-room

Second antechamber then cabinet of Madame de Pompadour. Cabinet (1768) then dining-room of Madame du Barry (1772). Billiard-room for Madame de Lamballe until 1786 when it became a dining-room. Second antechamber of Madame Élisabeth (1791). Antechamber of Cardinal Fesch (1804).

Decoration: the woodwork may have come from the cabinet of the Dauphin, the future Louis XVI, built in 1773 at the corner of the Stags Gallery and the former Orangery, projecting into the Diana garden (it was demolished in 1834). The mirrors were set in the panelling in 1863.

Furniture: many pieces of the First Empire furniture have been lost. Still in place are the pedestal table, the round table for the Emperor's lunch, Jacob-Desmalter, 1810; the wall-lights and fire-dogs, Thomire, 1810; the Louis-XVI Venus and Cupid clock and two candlesticks. The painted wood seats, covered with tapestry, come from the Tuileries and resemble those which were there in Napoléon's day.

The Emperor's second Drawing-room
(fig. 177)

Madame de Lamballe's second drawing-room in 1786. Noblemen's Chamber or Madame Élisabeth's Great Cabinet (1791). Cardinal Fesch's drawing-room (1804).

Decoration: pictures set in the panels in 1862: F. Boucher, *Jupiter and Callisto* and *Amyntas and Sylvia*; N.N. Coypel, *Bacchus and Ariadne*; C. Belle, *Psyche and Cupid asleep*; J.M. Vien, *Children playing with Swans*.

Furniture: installed in 1810, it is almost complete. Gilded wood seats upholstered in green cut velvet (chairs stamped Brion), 1810

(fig. 178). Savonnerie type carpet, Bellanger, 1810. Pedestal table, Jacob-Desmalter, 1810. Wall-lights, candlesticks and fire-dogs, Thomire, 1810. Giltwood side-tables with figures, Marcion, one of 1808, the other 1810. Chandelier, Chaumont, 1809. Clock made in 1810 by the clockmaker Lepaute, set in a small temple of precious marbles taken from a large "*surtout de dessert*" (tablecentre) made in Madrid at Buen Retiro *circa* 1791, and offered to Napoléon I by King Charles IV of Spain in Bayonne in 1808 (fig. 179). Candelabra belonging to the same "*surtout*".

178.
Chair and armchair in giltwood upholstered in green cut velvet, 1810.

177. The Emperor's second drawing-room.

Bedroom
of Méneval (fig. 180)
and the Emperor's
Wardrobe

Together with the following room, this took the place of the King's gamesroom as it existed from 1769 to 1782, before becoming Madame de Lamballe's drawing-room from 1783 to 1787. Then these mezzanine rooms were intended for Madame Élisabeth's servants. Lodging of Bacler d'Albe, the geographer in charge of Napoléon's topographical office (1807).

The bedroom, later occupied by Baron de Méneval, Keeper of the Emperor's Portfolio, was reconstitued in 1976 with furniture similar to that described in the inventory of 1810.

In the next-door wardrobe room, shelves by Jacob-Desmalter, 1810: a Shepherd-type mahogany toilet-seat (so-called from the name of the manufacturer who made it), installed for Madame Adélaïde.

Room for
the Keeper
of the Emperor's
Portfolio

Madame Élisabeth's inner cabinet (1791). In 1810 this room was occupied day and night by one of the two keepers of the Portfolio, Haugel and Landoire, who relayed

180.
Bedroom of Méneval,
Secrétaire du Portefeuille to Napoléon.

each other every twenty-four hours. According to Baron Fain, these ushers handed over the documents arriving for the Emperor. They opened the doors only to the secretaries and were responsible for the maintenance of the offices.

Their room was reconstituted in 1975 with very plain furniture.

The Emperor's
Bedchamber (fig. 181)

In 1786 this was Madame de Lamballe's Billiard-room. Madame Élisabeth's bedroom (1791). Cardinal Fesch's bedroom (1804).

Decoration: late 18th-century panelling. The alcove was removed in 1810. Chimney in brocatello marble. Overall restoration, 1977.

Furniture: the bed and seats were first placed in the Emperor's bedchamber on the first floor, before being moved here in 1810. Bronzed and giltwood bed with Egyptian figures, attributed to Jacob Frères (used by Pope Pius VII at the Tuileries in 1804-1805 before entering Fontainebleau in 1805). Canopy, Jacob-Desmalter, 1804 (embellished with laurel crowns and helmets in 1810). A bergère armchair, four armchairs, two chairs, attributed to Jacob Frères. Sofa, Jacob-Desmalter, 1806. After 1858 the whole set was upholstered in "chiné" velvet with wreaths of fruit and laurel branches (Grand Frères, 1811-1813) and with green taffeta rewoven in 1977. The screen has kept its Louis-XVI chiné velvet (Pernon, 1787) which was used to cover it in the First Empire. Pedestal table, Jacob-Desmalter, Bed-table, Jacob-Desmalter, 1810. Fire-dogs, Thomire, 1810. Candelabra with vestals, from the *surtout* offered by Charles IV, Madrid, Buen Retiro. Altar-clock in marble adorned with elements taken from the same *surtout*, Lepaute, 1810. Commode, bought for this room in 1810 from the dealer Rocheux. During the First Empire, the famous one in lacquer due to Martin Carlin, which came from Madame Victoire's Grand cabinet at Bellevue (Louvre), stood in its place.

181. The Emperor's bedchamber.

Intermediary room

(fig. 182)

Louis XVI's lathe cabinet (1786). Cardinal Fesch's cabinet (1804).

Decoration: wood panelling dating from Louis XV, apparently placed there in 1786 and stripped in 1863. Most of it comes from the king's retreat on the first floor, dating from 1736 and demolished in 1785. The overdoors by Lancret, installed in 1839, were sent to the Louvre in 1889 and replaced with poor copies.

Furniture: this room was refurnished for Napoléon in 1808, at the same time as the neighbouring ones. It was then a dispatch room. Except for the bronze fire-dogs, nothing remains of this furniture.

The Emperor's offices: third room

This room comes after the King's Billiard-room and has office furniture similar to that described in the 1810 inventory.

The Emperor's offices: second room

Louis XVI's Billiard-room (1786). Billiard-room of the Grand Maréchal (1804).

182. Intermediary room.

Furniture: in 1904 furniture from the former bedroom of Madame Mère was installed here, part of it was sent elsewhere in 1882 and then given to the Musée Napoléon by Madame Dumaine. Purple and yellow satin hangings, 1806. Mahogany and gilt bronze bed, Jacob-Desmalter, 1806. Bergères, armchairs and chairs in mahogany, Marcion, 1806. Commode, Jacob Frères, bought in 1804. Mahogany pedestal table from Madame Mère's first drawing-room.

The Emperor's offices: first room

François I bathroom. First half of Louis XVI's dining-room (1786).

Decoration: Louis-XVI period cornice, completed during the First Empire. Chimney installed in 1862. Various paintings set in the panels in 1862: *Concert of Birds* by F. Snyders (fig. 183); *Bird of Prey swooping on wild Ducks on a Marsh*, by Fyt; *Birds and two Hares*, anon.; *Parrot, white Pheasant and Spoonbill*, anon.; set of twelve anonymous canvases representing falcons; two studies, *Ducks and Eagles*, by P. Boel.

Furniture: office furniture recalling the intended use of this room. Mahogany chairs, Jacob Frères. Roll-top desk, Jacob-Desmalter, 1806. Wall-lights with a single branch, Duverger, 1808.

183. Snyders, *Concert of Birds.*

Antechamber "du Col de cygne"

François I steam bathroom. Louis XVI's buffet room (1786).

Decoration: gilt lead fountain representing a child playing with a swan among reeds, above a marble basin in the form of a seashell. This fountain, which gives the room its name, was executed in 1784 by the sculptor Roland and the chaser Thomire (fig. 184).

Showcase: set of Sèvres porcelain (fig. 185), with a crimson camaieu design consisting of garlands of flowers and bows of ribbon, used by both Louis XV and Louis XVI at Fontainebleau (pieces dated between 1756 and 1787, as some were replaced).

Topographical room

Second half of Louis XVI's dining-room (1786).

Decoration: Louis-XVI cornice, completed during the First Empire. Five overdoors in grisaille, three by Sauvage, 1786, two by Lussigny (*Fate* and *Victory*), 1810. The room was altered in 1862 (chimney moved, false door made), in order to receive the Hubert Robert pictures of the *Antiquities of Languedoc* (sent to the Louvre in 1889).

Furniture: several of the pieces of furniture found in this room in Napoléon's time have been removed, notably the two famous wardrobes by Boulle (now in the Musée du Louvre). Others have been put back: three

184.
Fountain in the "Col de cygne" antechamber, by Roland and Thomire, 1784.

186.
Geographical clock by Antide Janvier, 1791.

185. Sèvres porcelain service used by Louis XV and Louis XVI at Fontainebleau, 1756-1787.

tables serving to spread out the maps, Jacob-Desmalter; the Louis-XVI roll-top desk attributed to Riesener; the geographical clock by the famous clockmaker Janvier, indicating the time at every moment in each point in France, 1791, bought in 1806 (fig. 186); two wall-lights with arrow motifs; the gilt bronze fire-dogs, Ravrio, 1808; the carpet, Bellanger, 1810 (emblems changed during the Restoration).

Other furniture: two mahogany armchairs with female sphinxes and inlays, Jacob Frères; mahogany chairs with railed back, Jacob-Desmalter; mahogany desk chair, Marcion, 1806.

The Empress's Study

This room was occupied by the Duc de La Rochefoucauld (1705). The King's dining-room (1737). Madame Adélaïde's bedroom (1752). Madame Adélaïde's Great cabinet (1776). The King's gamesroom (1783). Madame Royale's Noblemen's Room (1786). Dining-room of Madame de La Rochefoucauld, lady-in-waiting to the Empress (1807). Intermediary room or dining-room (1808).

Decoration: the room acquired its present size when the façade was first moved forward into the Diana garden in 1751 and with the creation in 1773 of the rotunda. Elements of the woodwork date from Louis XV. Cornice, 1773 (?). Transformations in the Second Empire period: carved overdoors, mirror frames, rosace ceiling decoration, Huber, 1859; installation of an ancient mantlepiece.

Furniture: mahogany chairs, Jacob Frères, brought from the Empress's library at the Tuileries in 1808. Two table armchairs in mahogany adorned with bronzes, Marcion, 1809 (fig. 187). Two semicircular side-tables with figures and inlays, Jacob Frères, entered in 1804. Pedestal table with mosaic marble top, Jacob-Desmalter, 1807. Athénienne table, Jacob-Desmalter, 1809. Drawing table (fig. 188), inkstand, easel, Jacob-Desmalter, 1810; embroidery frame, Maigret, 1810 (for Marie-Louise). Tric-trac table, Louis-XVI period. Seven Sèvres vases, four of them flower-pots and three in Medici shape, Consulate period. Chandelier, Chaumont, 1809. Fire-dogs, Louis-XVI period. Wall-lights with arrows and lion's head motifs, Ravrio, 1808.

187.
Armchair
by Marcion, 1809.

188.
Drawing table by Jacob-Desmalter, 1810.

Boudoir or passage room leading to the garden

Pleated hangings in green taffeta, 1808 (re-done in 1827). Alcove sofa, chairs, Jacob-Desmalter, 1808. Alabaster lamp with gil-ded swan's necks, Chaumont, 1809.

The Empress's bedchamber (fig. 189)

Madame Adélaïde's Great cabinet (1752). Madame Adélaïde's bedroom (1776). The King's Billiard-room (1783). Madame Royale's bedroom (1786). Cardinal Caprara's

189. The Empress's bedchamber.

190. Commode by Thomire, 1809, reusing some bronzes from an older commode which had belonged to Madame Bonaparte.

191. Bedside table, delivered by Jacob-Desmalter in 1804.

bedroom (1804). Madame de La Rochefoucauld's drawing-room (1807).

Decoration: 18th-century cornice. Ancient mantlepiece placed here in 1859. Overdoor, mirror frames, ceiling rosace, Huber, 1859.

Furniture: wall hangings and curtains, lapis lazuli blue and white satin, brocaded in gold with rosettes, Lyon, Grand Frères, 1808. State bed and seats in gilded wood, Jacob-Desmalter, 1808 (the bed was enlarged in 1843 for Princess Clémentine and her husband, the Duke of Saxe-Coburg-Gotha). Savonnerie-type carpet, Bellanger, 1809. Pedestal "athénienne" table with a bronze tripod, Jacob-Desmalter, 1809. Mahogany commode, Thomire, 1809: some of the bronzes were taken from a piece of furniture made by the Jacob brothers which had belonged to Madame Bonaparte, Rue de la Victoire (fig. 190). Bedside table adorned with the figure of a sleeping dog, Jacob-Desmalter, 1804 (fig. 191). Wall-lights, candlesticks and fire-dogs with figures of Fame, Thomire, 1809. Clock, Terpsichore et Erato, Lepaute movement, 1809. Sèvres vases, Consulate period.

192.
The Empress's bathroom.

The Empress's bathroom (fig. 192)

Second antechamber of Mesdames (Louis XV's daughters), (1752). Madame Adélaïde's private boudoir (1776). Madame Royale's cabinet (1786). Second antechamber of Cardinal Caprara (1804). Madame de La Rochefoucauld's bedroom (1807).

Decoration: 18th-century cornice. Louis-XV panelling. Louis-XV chimneypiece placed here in 1859. Mirror frame and ceiling rosace, Huber, 1859.

Furniture: long draped curtains in sky-blue taffeta with a chamois-coloured braid, reconstituted in 1977. Sofa on a platform which can be pulled forward revealing a sunken bath, four gondola armchairs and two gondola chairs, fire-screen, all in giltwood, Jacob-Desmalter, 1808-1809, covered in sky-blue gourgouran rewoven in 1977. Savonnerie-type carpet, Bellanger, 1809 (emblems changed at the Restoration). Secrétaire in yew-wood (fig. 193), cheval glass and dressing table in mahogany richly adorned with bronzes, Thomire, 1809. Wall-lights, candlesticks, fire-dogs embellished with dancing women, Thomire, 1809. Chandelier, Chaumont, 1809. Two pairs of Sèvres vases, Consulate period. Portable dressing glass, Biennais, 1804. Clock with figure of Cupid lying in a basket, Lepaute movement, 1807, placed here during the Restoration.

193.
Secrétaire delivered by Thomire in 1809.

Passage or service room

Madame Victoire's great cabinet (1754). Madame Victoire's private cabinet (1771). Bedroom of the "sous-gouvernante" of the royal children (1783).

Decoration: refurbished in 1859 (creation of an alcove; cornice, mirror frames, overdoor panels, ceiling rosace, Huber; installation of an older chimneypiece).

Furniture: among the 1808-1809 furnishings the following are extant: the carpet, Bellanger, 1809; the very fine commode in citron and amaranthus wood with an inlaid figure of Isis, Jacob Frères, sold by Jacob-Desmalter in 1809 (fig. 194); pedestal table, Jacob-Desmalter, 1809; chandelier in the shape of a Chinese parasol, Chaumont, 1809; two wall-lights, Louis-XVI period; two candlesticks; Sèvres biscuit clock representing Astronomy, Lepaute movement, 1809; fire-dogs ornamented with griffins.

The G. Jacob seats which came from Comte d'Artois' turkish boudoir left the palace in 1846. The richly carved pieces of furniture executed by G. Jacob, seen here today (entered Fontainebleau in 1810 for the new Princes wing) evoke the former furniture.

194.
Commode by Jacob Frères, *c.* 1800.

The Empress's second drawing-room

(fig. 195)

This has taken the place of two rooms occupied in 1754 by Mesdames Sophie and Victoire, the first one being Madame Victoire's bedroom, the second one, Madame Sophie's bedroom, then in 1769, Madame Victoire's private room. Second antechamber and bedroom of Madame Royale, (1783). These two rooms were joined to form the great cabinet of the Dauphin and the Duc de Normandie. Drawing-room of Prince Joseph Bonaparte (1804).

Decoration: only the cornice goes back to the 18th century. The rest of the decoration was redone in 1859 (ceiling rosace, mirror frames, overdoor panels in Louis-XVI style, Huber; an ancient chimneypiece was installed).

Furniture: wall hangings in gros de Naples with a yellow ground embroidered with amaranth silk, bought from Boulard the upholsterer, 1808. Three sofas, two bergères, six armchairs, sixteen chairs, three footstools, a fire-screen, all in giltwood, Jacob-Desmalter, 1808. Two giltwood side-tables (the largest is fitted with two bronze pilasters at the back to protect it from the heat issuing from the hot air vent), Jacob-Desmalter, and bronzes by Thomire representing the Triumph of Trajan from a drawing by Antoine Dupasquier, 1808. Two jardinière tables, Jacob-Desmalter, with bronze ornaments by Thomire, 1808 (the baskets were re-used) (fig. 196). Two pedestal tables, Jacob Frères (bought in 1809). Carpet, Bellanger, 1809. Gilt-bronze chandelier with eighteen lights, Chaumont, 1809. Two gilt-bronze candelabra with an antique dancing girl mounted on a pedestal, Thomire, 1809 (fig. 197). Six wall-lights with children, candlesticks with Egyptian figures, card-table covered lamp, fire-dogs representing Psyche seated on an antique lamp, Thomire, 1809. Two large vases in Sèvres porcelain, Consulate period (fig. 198). Clock representing Time encircling the Universe, Lepaute movement, 1804.

195. The Empress's large drawing-room or yellow drawing-room.

196.
Jardinière on a side-table
by Jacob-Desmalter and Thomire, 1809.

197.
Candelabrum
by Thomire, 1809.

198.
Vase in Sèvres porcelain,
Consulate period.

The Empress's first drawing-room or Billiard-room

Madame Louise's bedroom (1754). Madame Sophie's bedroom (1769). Second antechamber of the Dauphin (1783). Bedroom of the Duc de Normandie (1786). Bedroom of Prince Joseph Bonaparte (1804).

Decoration: 18th-century ceiling cornice and panelling. Mirror frames, ceiling decoration, Huber, 1859.

Furniture: draped curtains in white taffeta with a green braid remade in 1974. Some of the seats (covered with purple gourgouran rewoven in 1973) from the 1808-1810 furnishings still remain: six giltwood chairs, two man's and two woman's "voyeuse" chairs (for watching card games), (fig. 199), (Jacob Frères) and four mahogany chairs, formerly in the second drawing-room of the Empress at the Tuileries; large sofa in gilded wood. Mahogany side-table, Jacob-Desmalter, 1805. Clock with the Three Graces in Sèvres biscuit after a model by the sculptor Chaudet, Lepaute movement, 1809. Gilded wood torchbearers, Louis-XVI period, from the Tuileries Palace, restored by Thomire in 1809. Gilt bronze wall-lights, Duverger, 1810. Candlesticks and fire-dogs by Thomire, 1809. Savonnerie carpet, Louis-XV period (fig. 200), formerly in the Empress's first drawing-room at the Tuileries. The billiard table, delivered by Duplessis in 1810, has been lost.

Passage

Antechamber shared by Madame Sophie and Madame Louise (1769). The Dauphin's cabinet (1783). Noblemen's room for the Royal children (1786). During the First Empire, this passage served as a storeroom for card tables (from the first drawing-room).
Mahogany chairs, Jacob Frères. Low cabinet in mahogany, Jacob Frères, entered in 1804. Three *quadrille* tables, Louis-XVI period. Mahogany *bouillotte* table, Empire period.

The Empress's antechamber

Madame Louise's bedroom (1769). Madame Sophie's bedroom (1771). The Dauphin's bedroom (1783).

Decoration: cornice and wood panelling, 1769. Panelling in the alcove, 1773. Mirror frame, overdoor panels, 1859.

Furniture: plain cotton curtains made in 1974. Four benches from the 1808 furnishings. Gilt bronze lantern, Duverger, 1806.

199.
Lady's "voyeuse" chair by Jacob Frères.

200.
Savonnerie carpet, 18th century.

201. Stags Gallery.

Stags Gallery

(fig. 201)

History: seventy-four metres long and seven metres wide, it was decorated around 1600 with distant views of royal forests and residences, painted in oil on plaster and wrongly attributed in the 18th century to Toussaint Dubreuil. They are actually due to the painter Louis Poisson (+ 1613), born in Gisors, who was also responsible, according to the royal accounts, for the views in the Roe Gallery and those of towns in the King's Gallery at the new Château de Saint-Germain-en-Laye, both destroyed. On the window side and between the views opposite there were stags' heads (forty-three of them in 1642) between the views, hence its name. The antlers alone were natural and here and there some labels indicated the dates when the stags had been taken. One of the antlers, situated near the view of Compiègne, belonged to a stag which killed Saint-Bon, one of the king's huntsmen, on 14 October 1608 in the forest of Sénart. The lower part of the walls was panelled.

As early as 1639, the twenty-two large ceiling beams had given way and had to be replaced. Pierre Poisson (+1643), Louis' son, decorated them with hunting trophies including boar's and wolf's heads, hunting horns, spears and arquebuses. He also restored the mural paintings and painted the three new doors leading from the gallery to the garden. In 1679, the floor was given a new paving of stone from Caen and hard limestone.

In the 18th century the gallery was considerably altered. In 1769, in order to enlarge the apartment of King Louis XV's daughters, situated beneath the royal apartments, a cabinet was created for Madame Louise in the first two bays on the side of the Oval Courtyard. In 1770, to enable the Dauphin, lodged on the ground floor overlooking the moat at the other end of the gallery, to reach the Dauphine Marie-Antoinette's apartment (that is to say in the Queen's apartments) more easily, the ceiling was knocked down and a staircase was built near Madame Louise's cabi-

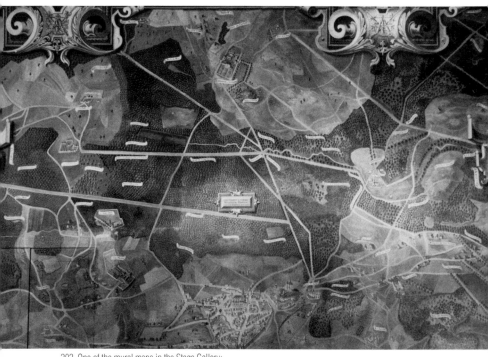

202. One of the mural maps in the Stags Gallery:
the Château de Saint-Léger and the Town of Montfort surrounded by the Forest.

net, blocking four windows. In Louis XVI's reign, the plans of the Château in 1783 reveal that the gallery was further impeached upon with the installation of two Billiard-rooms. Finally, in 1786, the King decided to sacrifice the whole of the gallery to provide more room for his children and their service. The forty-six stag's heads were removed and placed beneath the terrace of the Fountain Courtyard (the antlers were deposited in the chapel during the Revolution) and the space was divided up. However these operations were never finished and it was Napoléon who, in 1806-1807, completed them by creating three apartments for princes.

This situation lasted until 1860. Napoléon III then decided to reinstate the gallery to provide easier access to the apartments on the Princes Courtyard. In the course of the demolition works, the architect Paccard found the ceiling almost intact and many fragments of the mural decoration. He therefore proposed to restitute the original decor.

The Emperor hesitated, for he had thought of installing the tapestries of the "Mois des Maisons Royales" there, but Paccard finally had his way. Work began in 1865, entailing much research in the collections of maps and plans held in archives and libraries, and lasted until 1868. Paccard called upon Alexander Denuelle (1818-1879) for all the decorative painting: beams, girders, frieze, pier bays with stag's heads, castles and houses appearing in the middle of maps. Denuelle was assisted by several other artists: Lameire, Guifard, Nicolle, Bernard, Loridan, Cornet, Quatremaire, Marre. Moreover, Jacques Guiaud (1811-1876) was put in charge of the wide views of forests, Félix-Hippolyte Lanoue (1812-1872) was responsible for the small camaieu landscapes. Léon Dumont-Tournel provided the "Middle Ages" stained glass, Ducros, the wrought-iron railing at the south end, Desachy, twenty stags' heads in staff with enamel eyes modelled on the heads on the Diana fountain.

203. The Château de Folembray.

The original panelling was not reconstituted, but copies were made of the decoration in the upper Saint-Saturnin chapel and a parquet floor was laid.

In the 20th century, under the direction of the architect R. de Cidrac, the painted decoration was again restored, by M. Ledeur and his team. A stone and terracotta paving replaced the parquet floor.

Though banquets, plays, concerts, etc. were often held in the gallery, it is famous above all for an event which took place there on 10 November 1657, when the Marquis of Monaldeschi, Queen Christina of Sweden's Master of the Horse, was assassinated at the command of the Queen herself. The victim, accused of being a traitor, was murdered in cold blood by the captain of the Queen's guards and two hired killers. The Queen, who had asked the prior of the Mathurin monastery to come and receive Monaldeschi's confession, did not waver. This event has long continued to cause amaze-

ment. In the 19th century it inspired many writers (Brault, Soulié, Alexandre Dumas) and artists (Delacroix, Ouvrié, Lesage, Madame Grandpierre-Deverzy).

Mural decoration: the wall on the Oval Courtyard side, on entering: view of Saint-Germain-en-Laye (completely redone in the 19th century). On the wall opposite the windows are found in succession: the Château de Madrid and the Bois de Boulogne, the Château de Verneuil and the forest of Halatte, the Château de Montceaux-en-Brie and the surrounding forest, the Château de Charleval and the forest of Lyons, the Château de Saint-Léger, the town and forest of Montfort-l'Amaury (fig. 202), the Château, town and forest of Blois, the Château, town and forest of Villers-Cotterêts, the Château, town and forest of Compiègne, the Châteaux de Folembray (fig. 203) and Coucy and their forest. On the end wall, the Château and forest of Fontainebleau (entirely redone in the 19th cen-

tury). On the window side, the Château du Bois de Vincennes and the great plan for the Louvre and the Tuileries drawn up in Henri IV's time.

Sculptures: since 1967, the Département des Sculptures of the Musée du Louvre has given back to the Musée de Fontainebleau one group, seven statues and two busts in bronze which had been removed from the Château during the Revolution and sent to the Muséum central des Arts. Among the large sculptures, five had been cast at Fontainebleau itself, between 1541 and 1543, under the direction of Primaticcio and with the participation of Vignole, from hollowed moulds obtained by Primaticcio from marble statues in Rome. They are *Laocoon and his Sons*, a group after a marble copy made in the 1st century A.D. (Vatican) of a Hellenistic original (Rhodes) of the 2nd century B.C. (placed in the Queen's garden from the 16th century – no later than 1565 – until the end of the 18th century); *Venus*, after an antique copy in marble (Vatican) of the Venus of Cnidus by Praxiteles, 4th century B.C. (placed between 1570 and 1646 [?] in a niche of the façade of the wing called the Fine Chimney wing, and later in the Queen's garden);

204.
After the Antique,
Hercules and Telephus,
between 1541 and 1543.

205.
After the Antique,
Ariadne sleeping.

Apollo of the Belvedere after a Roman copy in marble (Vatican) of a Greek statue of the 4th century B.C. (in the same places as the *Venus*); *Hercules and Telephus*, called *Hercules Commodus* (fig. 204), after a Roman copy (Vatican) of a Greek statue of the 4th century B.C. (in the same places as the *Venus* and *Apollo*); *Ariadne sleeping*, once known as *Cleopatra* (fig. 205) after a Roman copy of the 2nd century A.D. (Vatican) from a Hellenistic original (Pergamon) around 200 B.C. (from about 1565 to around 1600 in the Queen's garden, then in the Grand parterre and, from 1646 [?] onwards, again in the Queen's garden). The three other statues preserved represent *Mercury*, after an antique marble (Florence), cast in the 16th century, perhaps at Fontainebleau (in the same places as the *Venus*, *Apollo* and *Hercules*); *Diana with a Doe*, a copy made in 1602 by Barthélemy Prieur of a Roman marble statue (Louvre) given by Pope Paul IV to Henri II (in 1556) and placed in the Queen's garden, itself a copy of an original Hellenistic bronze (main element of the new Diana fountain in the Queen's garden created by Francini in 1603, on which it was placed until the Revolution); and finally, *The Scythian Flayer* known as the *Knife-Grinder* or *Rotator* or *Arrotino*, no doubt executed in 1688 by the Napolitan caster Guiseppe Vinacci, after a Roman replica in marble (Florence) of a Hellenistic original (Pergamum) approximately 210-200 B.C., which is part of the group of the Sacrifice of Marsyas (replacing the *Tireur d'Epine* (boy pulling out a thorn) in the Queen's garden around 1690). The two busts situated at the end of the gallery are found mentioned for the first time in 1642, when they adorned the niches of the inner façade of the Dauphine Gate. They date from the 16th century, but their origin is unknown. One represents Tiberius and the other a crowned priest, both from the Antique.

Decorative art: in a showcase the sword and coat of mail belonging to Monaldeschi (fig. 206) are on display, which the Trinitarian or Mathurin monks kept until the Revolution in their treasure room. They passed to the Ecole centrale de Seine-et-Marne, then in 1803 to the Ecole spéciale militaire, in 1808 to Saint-Cyr, during the Second Empire to the Musée d'Artillerie at Saint-Thomas d'Aquin, then to the Tuileries. Napoléon III, who had claimed them for his arms museum, sent them back to Fontainebleau before 1865.

206.
Sword and coat of mail which belonged to Monaldeschi.

Queen's Staircase

In the 17th century, Guardroom of Monsieur, Louis XIV's brother. 1745, first antechamber of the Dauphine. 1768, the Queen's staircase.

Erected in 1768 to replace the former 16th-century stairs lodged in the portico. The door casings and the wrought-iron balustrade with the monogram MA, probably of Marie Leszczynska, who died before the work was finished. In 1838-1839 Louis-Philippe changed the look of this staircase by having a painted and gilded coffered ceiling placed above it, with pictures set in the walls painted in imitation marble. The pictures chosen by Louis-Philippe evoke hunting: two canvases by F. Desportes, *Boar stopped by eight Hounds* and *Death of a Wolf*, 1702 (fig. 207) (from the gallery in the new château at Meudon); J.B. Oudry, *Stag Hunting in the Oise, View of Compiègne near Royallieu*, 1737 (tapestry cartoon for the hangings representing the *Hunts of Louis XV*, woven at the Gobelins factory); Oudry studio, *Wolf attacked by six Hounds* (the 1724 original is at Ansbach); 18th-century French school, *Still Life and Game*, *Game guarded by two Hounds* and *Dog chasing two Ducks*.

Six gilt bronze brackets for a carcel lamp, Chaumont, 1840.

207.
François Desportes,
Death of a Wolf,
1702.

Hunts
apartment

The apartment is situated in a building erected around 1601 by Henri IV. In 1625 the Pope's legate, Cardinal Barberini, was lodged here. Mazarin apparently lived in it during the Régence period, then Monsieur, the King's brother and his wife during the reign of Louis XIV. In the 18th century, after the death of the Princesse Palatine, it was occupied in succession by Cardinal de Fleury in 1743, Madame de Lauraguais and Madame de Flavacourt in 1744, the first Dauphine, Marie-Thérèse-Raphaelle of Spain in 1745, Queen Marie Leszczynska in 1746 (while work was being done on her own apartment), the new Dauphine Marie-Josèphe de Saxe from 1747 until her death in 1767 (in 1749 Madame Élisabeth, Duchess of Parma, Louis XV's eldest daughter, stayed here on a visit to her parents). In 1767, Maréchal d'Estrées and Comtesse de Coigny lived here and in 1768, King Christian VII of Denmark. Then in 1773 the King decided to give it to the Comtesse d'Artois, her husband occupying the corresponding apartment on the ground floor, which was that of his father the Dauphin.

Many people passed through in the 19th century: in 1804 Baron de Dalberg, Arch-chancellor of the German Empire, in 1807 Marie-Julie Clary, Queen of Naples; during the Restoration the Duc de Bourbon, then the Duc d'Angoulême when he came to hunt in the forest of Fontainebleau. During the July Monarchy, the Duc d'Orléans, then from 1833 the Duc d'Aumale and the Duc de Montpensier were entitled to this apartment, but temporary occupants came to stay, according to circumstances: in May 1837 it was the hereditary Grand Dowager Duchess of Mecklenburg-Schwerin, Augusta of Hesse-Homburg with Princess Helen, her daughter-in-law (before her marriage); in 1838, Duke Alexander of Würtemberg, his wife Princesse Marie, the King's daughter, and their son; in 1844 the Duchess of Kent, Queen Victoria's mother; in 1845, the Prince and Princesse de Joinville; in 1846, the Prince

and Princess of Salerno, the Duc d'Aumale's parents-in-law.

The situation changed with the Second Empire. Though in 1853 it was occupied by the Prince (Lucien) and Princesse Murat, in 1856 it was reserved for the Prince Imperial from the day he was born, as it was close to the Empress's apartments. The Prince lived there until 1868.

The Prince Imperial's drawing-room

In the 17th century, antechamber of Monsieur. 1745, second antechamber of the Dauphine. 1774, Guardroom of the Comtesse d'Artois; 1805, antechamber of the Duc de Bourbon. 1835, antechamber of the Duc d'Aumale and the Duc de Montpensier. 1856, the Prince Imperial's drawing-room.

Decoration: nothing remains of the 18th-century decoration apart from the chimney in Languedoc marble, installed in 1744. The large pictures of the *Hunts of Louis XV* by Oudry were set in the walls in 1835, the other pictures (between the windows and on the overdoors) were hung in the following years: J.B. Oudry, *Pack of Hounds running towards the Meeting Point at the Embrassade Crossroads, Forest of Compiègne*, 1743; also by Oudry, *Louis XV holding a Hound, entering the Wood, at the Lonely Well Crossroads in the Forest of Compiègne*, 1739, and *Rendez-vous at the King's Well Crossroads, Forest of Compiègne*, called *Le Botter*, 1735 (fig. 208): in the centre is the Comte de Toulouse on horseback, on the King's right, M. de Beringhen, First Equerry, on the King's left, Prince Charles de Lorraine, Master of the Horse; J.J. Bachelier, *Antler of a Stag caught in the Forest of Compiègne, 1 July 1767* (fig. 209); by the same, *Antlers of a Stag attacked at the Haute-Queue in Compiègne Forest, 5 July 1764*. Three overdoors: French school, 17th century. *Birds gathered near a Marsh;*

208.
Jean-Baptiste Oudry,
Rendez-vous at the Puits-du-Roi Crossroads,
Forest of Compiègne,
called *Le Botter,*
1735.

French school, 18th century. *Dog, Parrot and Parakeets*; Desportes (attributed to), *Boar facing up to Hounds*.

Furniture: as in the Second Empire (reconstituted in 1974). Giltwood seats, stamped Marcion, including a settee, six armchairs, six chairs, a screen, placed in 1818 in Louis XVIII's bedchamber at Saint-Cloud, covered since 1838 with a crimson, yellow-patterned damask (entered in 1856). Console in black wood, stamped Jacob Frères (entered in 1804). Mahogany table with side flaps, Second Empire period (entered 1860). Astronomy and Geometry clock, movement by Manière, early 19th century (entered 1864). Candelabra with female figures, Thomire, 1812 for the Elysée (likewise entered in 1864). Fire-dogs, late 18th century (bought from Baudouin, 1804).

209.
Jean-Jacques Bachelier,
*Antler of a Stag caught
in Compiègne Forest,
1 July 1767.*

The Prince Imperial's bedroom

In the 17th century, Monsieur's bedroom. 1745, the Dauphine's Great cabinet. 1774, Comtesse d'Artois' Noblemen's Room. 1805, dining-room of Prince Joseph, King of Naples. 1814, dining-room of the Duc de Bourbon. 1833, Billiard-room of the Duc d'Aumale and the Duc de Montpensier. 1856, the Prince Imperial's bedroom.

Decoration: executed in 1744. Some elements of the panelling, the ceiling ornaments (restored in the 19th century) and the Serrancolin marble chimney have remained. As in the preceding room, the large paintings of the *Hunts of Louis XV* by Oudry were set in the wall panelling in 1835, pictures were hung between the windows in 1836 and the overdoors in 1837: J.B. Oudry, *The old Pack of Hounds unleashed at the Petite Patte d'Oie Intersection, Forest of Compiègne*, called *The Relay*, 1741; by the same artist, *Stag at Bay among the Franchard Rocks, Forest of Fontainebleau*, 1738 (fig. 210) (the artist can be discerned, bottom right) (fig. 211); again by the same artist, *Death of a Stag at the Pond of Saint-Jean-aux-Bois, Forest of Compiègne*, 1736 (fig. 210); by the same artist, *Strange Antlers of a Stag caught by the King at Fontainebleau in April 1742*; J.J. Bachelier, *Antlers of a Stag hunted by the King at Saint-Hubert, 10 June 1767*; Nicasius Bernaerts (called Nicasius), *Young Roe-deer* (from the Menagery at Versailles). Overdoors: French school, 18th century, two still lifes with game.

Furniture: as in the Second Empire. Bed and bedside table in mahogany, Fourdinois, 1864 (models repeated for the Prince Imperial in various palaces). Giltwood seats: eight armchairs and six chairs bought in 1810 for the first drawing-room of the Emperor's private apartment at Fontainebleau , gilded and placed in the Tuileries in Louis-Philippe's reign in the Duc d'Orléans' small drawing-room, the screen executed in 1819 for the second drawing-room (Peace Room) in the state apartments at the Tuileries Palace, the whole set being re-upholstered after 1837

Further reading

For a thorough knowledge of Fontainebleau, two fundamental early works are indispensable: Père Pierre Dan, *Le Trésor des Merveilles de la Maison royale de Fontainebleau...*, Paris, 1642, and Abbé Guilbert, *Description historique des château, bourg et forest de Fontainebleau...*, Paris, 1731, 2 vol. The best source of reference is still the monograph by Félix Herbet, *Le Château de Fontainebleau*, Paris, 1937, though many points need rectifying or completing. Concerning the XVIth century, the Galerie François I has been the subject of a collective study under the direction of André Chastel (Paris, Flammarion, 1972), an essential work to which may be added the book by S. Béguin, J. Guillaume and A. Roy on the former celebrated decoration, destroyed in the reign of Louis XV, of the Galerie d'Ulysse (Paris, Presses universitaires de France, 1985). Regarding the work undertaken by Henri IV, see *Le Château de Fontainebleau sous Henri IV*, Petit journal des grandes expositions n° 61, 1978. Many changes which took place at the time of Louis XV have been described in detail by Y. Bottineau in *L'Art d'Ange-Jacques Gabriel à Fontainebleau*, Paris, 1962 (see also a collective work: *Hommage aux Gabriel*, Paris, Picard, 1982).

The general guide which preceded the present one was written by B. Lossky, *Le Musée national du château de Fontainebleau*, Paris, Réunion des musées nationaux, 1971. Various small guides on particular aspects have been published since 1980 by the present author in collaboration with C. Samoyault-Verlet and have served as reference here. An album exists on the Musée Napoléon Ier, written by J.-P. Samoyault and C. Samoyault-Verlet, Paris, Editions des musées nationaux, 1986.

Table of contents

Plans

Photo Credits

Réunion des musées nationaux
(photographs by Arnaudet, Blot,
Lagiewski, Willi, Bernard)
2-4,6, 7, 9-11, 17, 19-22, 26, 28-30, 34, 35,
37, 39, 47-49, 51, 52, 55-57, 61, 63, 66, 68,
72, 77, 81, 83, 89, 91, 93, 96-98, 100, 101,
103-106, 108, 110, 113, 119-122, 124-126,
131, 132, 135-139, 142, 143, 157, 158, 160-
163, 166, 170, 171, 175, 179, 181, 185, 186,
195, 201, 207-209, 214-221, 223-233, 235-
237, 239-242
Musée national du Château de Fontainebleau
(photographs by Rigal, Esparcieux, Landin,
Roussel, Richard, Lagiewski)
5, 8, 12-16, 27, 32, 33, 36, 38, 41, 53, 54b,
60, 62, 64, 67, 69-71, 73-75, 78, 80, 84-88,
90, 92, 94, 95, 99, 102, 107, 109, 111, 115,
117, 123, 127, 130, 133, 134, 140, 141, 144-
152, 154-156, 159, 164, 165, 168, 169, 172-
174, 176-178, 180, 183, 187-194, 196-200,
202-206, 212, 222, 234, 238
Bibliothèque nationale
23, 25, 40, 44, 46, 50, 114, 118
Lauros-Giraudon 76, 82, 129, 210, 211
Caroline Rose 24, 116, 167, 182
Gérard Rondeau 65, 79, 213
Archives Phot-SPADEM 43, 112
Esparcieux 18, 184
Feuillie 128, 153
Archives nationales 1
Musée national du Château de Pau 45
Bulloz 54
Agence France-Presse 58
Studio Lourmel 31
Inventaire général Région Bourgogne 42

Printed in november 1993
by l'Imprimerie ❑ Alençonnaise in Alençon
from designs by Jean-Pierre Jauneau

L'Imprimerie ❑ Alençonnaise also composed
the text in Times and engraved the illustrations.
The paper was made by JOB

Dépôt légal : 1er trimestre 1994
N° d'ordre : 24197
ISBN: 2-7118-2454-3
GG 20 2454